Stop Asking Why Are You Single

(A Journey Towards Healing and Contentment in Christ)

Indiana Tuggle

Copyright © 2014 by Indiana Tuggle
Victory Publishing Inc.
P.O. Box 752584
Memphis, TN 38175

All rights reserved. No part of this publication may be reproduced, stored in a retrieval system, or transmitted in any form or by any means – electronic, mechanical, photocopy, recording, or any other – except for brief quotations in printed reviews, without prior permission.
All Scripture quotations unless otherwise marked are from New King James Version of the Bible, © 1979, 1980, 1982, 1990 by Thomas Nelson Inc.

Edited by Zipporah Williams, Memphis, TN.

ISBN 10: 0-9993411-0-0
ISBN 13: 978-0-9993411-0-0

Printed in the United States of America

Acknowledgements

To my Lord and Savior Jesus Christ, thank you for believing in me, choosing me for such a task, and encouraging me along the way.

To my brother, Prentiss King and my mother Deborah Tuggle thank you for always protecting me and being there for me. It is your love that has strengthened me over the years.

To my spiritual father, Bishop H.D. Vann, thank you for your integrity and modeling of true Christianity. It is through your unconditional love and kindness that I have learned to trust again.

To my Powerhouse family, thank you for teaching me the most important aspect about being a Christian, relationship with God. It is through this relationship that I have discovered who I am and who He is in me.

To my spiritual family: Mama Patricia Key, big sisters Jennifer Sample and Bobriller Hill and my little sister Zipporah Williams. Thank you for your support, encouragement and occasional kick in the butt to keep me on track.

Table of Contents

Introduction i
Chapter 1: Being Single is a Blessing Not a Curse! 7
Chapter 2: If I Don't Get Him/Her, I Will Still Praise Him 27
Chapter 3: He That Findeth 47
Chapter 4: Delight Yourself in the Lord! 63
Chapter 5: God's Work Not Busy Work 81
Chapter 6: Happiness Comes From God . 103
Chapter 7: Living in the Moment 125
Chapter 8: Enjoy Who You Are & Where You Are With God 143

Introduction

In my frustrations of being single and being asked by so many why I was still single, I posed that same question to God. His response was the inspiration for the book title as well as the eight chapters that encompass the book. God does not want us to question his plans for our journey rather He expects us to trust Him and walk in them.

Singleness is a journey that all must go through. But as I have learned "Frustration is a result of trying to do something in your own strength that only God can do." Only God can provide a suitable mate and will do so in His perfect timing. As Christians we can sulk and complain, in hopes to speed up the process, or in my case, in hopes that God will finally give in and give me what I want. This brings me to another lesson, "God does not do anything out of season." Therefore we must choose whether to go through with joy or with anguish. *Stop Asking Why Are You Single* is my journey through the frustrations of singleness into healing, true happiness and the joy of the Lord.

This book is not a complete guide, it is merely the beginning or the opening of the door to acknowledge and do the work that is required. It is intended for single Christians, male and female, who desire a mate and have let that desire consume their very being and hinder their relationship with God. It is also intended for Christians, who received a promise from the Lord and have become frustrated or their heart has hardened in the wait.

In each chapter I offer transparency into my struggles and afflictions of the past and present, as well as how I overcame, with the help of God. Each chapter represents deliverance from a particular area in my life. While writing this book, God led me to study four books of the bible: John, Romans, Ephesians and Matthew. Therefore the book is filled with prophetic revelations revealed by the Holy Spirit as I studied these books. This book also contains revelations from pastors, prophets, prophetesses, ministers, etc. through sermons and personal words of encouragement I have heard and received.

The book is divided into eight chapters; within those chapters are topics that were relevant to the chapter at hand. Some topics may seem to repeat in some chapters however with the changing chapter there is a new aspect of that particular topic. **Chapter 1: Being single is a blessing not a curse** tackles viewing ourselves through worldly standards, questioning God, focusing on what you don't have, living in the past and letting go and letting God (trust). In this chapter I learned how to stop comparing myself to a non-Christian world and to be grateful for what God has already done in my life. **Chapter 2: If I don't get him/her, I will still praise Him** tells how to cut the enemy off at the knees, recognizing what hinders your praise, and the importance of praise. Chapter two taught me to praise God no matter what because it is what He created us to do and it is what moves God to work on our behalf.

Chapter 3: He that findeth…tackles the act of searching for a mate in topics such as starting with God, looking for love in all the wrong places, letting go of the past (forgiveness) and seeking after God not man. In this chapter I discovered that there is nothing wrong with me. God's timing is not our timing and it is not my job to "physically find" my husband despite what the books and magazines say. **Chapter 4: Delight yourself in the Lord** discusses relinquishing your wants, with Christ life is just beginning, remember the word, comparing yourself to others, seeking advice from the ungodly, aborting the process, and serving God with expectations. Chapter 4 is generally about relationship with God and what is required to enhance that relationship. God wants us to focus on Him, pleasing Him and loving others in return He will focus on our needs.

Chapter 5: God's work not busy work focuses on living life on purpose with purpose and understanding what prevents us from drawing closer to God. God created us for a purpose; it is the fulfilling of that purpose that should guide our actions.

This chapter also taught me about the tricks of the enemy that prevent us from getting closer to God to discover our purpose such as loneliness, fear, identity issues, and disobedience. **Chapter 6: Happiness comes from God** provides guidance to true happiness such as recognizing who you are, believing His word, staying the course, watching what you say, staying in your lane (stop trying to do God's job), seeking to please the Lord, and fighting for your happiness. In this chapter I discovered true happiness is not in what you have but in who you are and when the enemy gets us to question who we are we are unable to be used by God.

Chapter 7: Living in the moment provides practical steps to let go of the past (acknowledging your feelings, releasing the blame, forgiving yourself and others, and realizing others need your help) and relinquishing control of the future by remembering the words spoken over you, trusting God's plan, realizing God is in control, staying in the word, and letting go of fear. This chapter also discusses being mindful of the present. Chapter 7 was basically a reminder of how far God has brought me. The most important thing I learned in this chapter is "God is not in our past pushing us through nor in our futures waiting for us to get to where He is, He is walking with us, beside us, in our present. To dwell on either the past or the future is to deny His power in our lives." Life is a continuous journey it will not end when we finally get our mate, God has so much for us and He is waiting to release it if we just trust Him.

Chapter 8: Enjoy who you are and where you are with God is an acknowledgement of who you are, whose you are and how to enjoy it. God does not hide our purpose from us; He reveals it to us when we ask. It is the very thing that we are most passionate about and would do it whether we got paid for it or not. Generally others recognize who we are or our purpose before we do. The power of God and the strength to accomplish it lies in our purpose. In this chapter I challenge the reader to write their purpose down and read it daily and then ask God how to accomplish it. Joy comes in completing each task rather than in the final product. Obedience is in completion, the results are up to God.

My hopes in writing *Stop Asking Why Are You Single*, is that sharing my struggles and my journey will encourage someone else in their own personal journey as well as challenge others to examine their relationship with God and start living the victorious life God promised for all His children. So many Christians are hurting and drowning in past mistakes which have paralyzed them from enjoying the fullness of God. God did not mean for us to merely survive, He wants us to THRIVE. God promised us many blessings in this journey called life, we cannot get discouraged because we don't have them when we want them or dwell on missing one over the other.

Chapter 1

Being Single is a Blessing Not a Curse!

Out of the fullness of His grace He has blessed us all, giving us one blessing after another.
John 1:16 (GNT)

I know that phrase may sound cliché and I know you've probably heard it a million times. But it is absolutely true. However we have a hard time accepting the truth when we don't believe it ourselves. Belief in this one simple fact is dependent upon the garbage that has been thrown at us by the environment we live.

Stop viewing yourself through worldly standards

This statement is important not only to understanding the blessing of being single, but to your Christian walk and relationship with God. Let's begin with the societal definition. The world defines single as being without a partner or significant other, or not being in a relationship. Though partially true (single is properly defined as not married); the problem is not in the definition but in the stigmatism associated with the definition. Single people are viewed as lonely, unhappy, unattractive, and/or unwanted. Why do we accept this? We are a product of our environment. It is what we were taught and what we see.

The first stage in puberty is marked by the first time we have feelings or likings for the opposite sex. I remember being taunted by friends saying "Indie got a boyfriend," or "Indie and so-and-so sitting in a tree k-i-s-s-i-n-g......"! What about the stories we grew up on? "Cinderella" and "Sleeping Beauty", depict the poor misfortunate, mistreated woman finally being rescued by her prince charming or knight in shining armor. Thus women grew up learning that a man was supposed to take care of them and rescue them from the big bad world. Men, on the other hand, grew up thinking that money, power and good looks would get them the woman of their dreams. Funny thing is the fairy tale always ended with the wedding and/or the couple riding off into the sunset. We never really saw "ever after", or better yet who taught the couple how to treat each other.

We also accept these false realities because we long to be in a relationship. Nothing wrong with that, its human nature, God created us that way. The problem comes when you cannot be or see yourself happy without it. Either you never start or you stop enjoying life and begin the "when I get" syndrome. When I get a boyfriend/girlfriend I want to travel more. When I get a boyfriend/girlfriend I want to go to this place or that place. When I get a boyfriend/girlfriend I am going to go to the movies every weekend. Truth be told, there are some things that you will begin to enjoy as a couple. But why can't you go and do now? If we wait until we find that special person, we will end up placing high performance expectations on that person and setting ourselves up for disappointment. Our whole lives are caught up in relationships. We begin to be envious of those in them. We flock to the tabloids to see what celebrity is dating whom. Then we begin to wonder why it has not happened for us. This can be dangerous because you can end up searching and finding an unhealthy relationship or settling for less than what God has for you.

Secondly, as I stated earlier, if one is single, they are viewed by society as lonely, mean, and something must be wrong with them. I remember I had a repair man over to my house to do some renovations. He came with a friend. We were in the house laughing and joking having a good time. Both of the men were looking around at the house complementing me on how nice it was decorated. Then one asked, "You live alone?" I replied "Yes, why?" He said "Do you have a boyfriend?" I said "No, why?" He said, "you seem like a pretty cool chick, cute, nice, no kids, own house; why don't you have a man?" We've all been asked this question, and to date, I still cannot come up with the appropriate answer to prevent the same response I always get. I've tried "Just haven't found Mr. Right" and "Waiting on God to send my husband". I've even tried sarcasm, "why you all up in my business." Regardless of my response I get: "Something must be wrong with you or you must be mean and hateful that no man will put up with you." So what is the best answer to this question? There is no perfect answer or response to get them off your back. You must have confidence in who you are and whose you are.

As single Christians we must remember that we are children of God. We are commissioned to live our lives in a Christ-like manner. Stop allowing the world to tell you that you are less than who you are. We are living in a world where God is a convenience. They take Him out or pray when they need something from Him and only follow the words in the bible that are suitable to them or their current situation. There is nothing wrong with you but everything wrong with the world. As Christians we are commissioned to live a life holy and acceptable unto Christ.

Do not love the world or the things in the world. If anyone loves the world, the love of the Father is not in him. For all that is in the world – the lust of the flesh, the lust of the eyes, and the pride of life – Is not of the Father but is of the world. And the world is passing away, and the lust of it; but he who does the will of God abides forever. -1 John 2: 15 – 17

But you already know this. The problem is not lack of knowledge. The problem is that behind closed doors you question yourself and God. What's wrong with me? Why am I single? Why haven't I met anyone? How long must I wait God? And then when you step outside the door, the unhappiness is written all over your face. The world begins to ask you those same questions, you can't handle it, you get angry, and you don't know what to say. Truth is, if you believed that you were blessed and not cursed you wouldn't be questioning God or afraid to face the world.

Side Note: for those who are saying, "I'm not questioning God, I'm questioning myself." If you are a Christian, you were bought with a price (the blood of Jesus); you are no longer your own entity, by questioning yourself you question He who lives in you and He who created you.

Stop questioning God

Ask any married person, happily or miserable, being single is not the worst thing in the world. Here you are focusing on one phase or aspect of your life when God is trying to bless you in other areas. God has not forgotten you. I don't claim to know everything there is to know about God and I am pretty sure that there is a lot yet to be seen. But what I do know is that God is a God of order. Everything will happen in His perfect timing. I have such a hard time with this one. As a single person and someone taking care of myself and doing for myself, one of the hardest things I had to believe about myself was I AM SPOILED. I mean I am an independent woman; I do what I want when I want. I work hard so I can have what I want when I want it. Problem is I treated God the same way. I prayed on Sunday and expected my blessing on Monday. Everything was urgent to me. And if God didn't deliver I took it to mean either He wasn't listening or I needed to handle it myself. "Wait" and "not right now" were not in my vocabulary.

I gave my life to Christ at a young age; needless to say I backslid and led a sinful life going from one relationship to another. In this last relationship, I remember this guy would often tell me I belonged to him and I would always reply "I belong to Jesus". If someone ever said God don't talk to sinners, I am living proof that is a lie. One day after making that statement, I clearly heard God say "if you belong to me prove it, let go of your sinful ways and follow me." When I heard that I begin to argue with God. I was completing my bachelor's degree, the guy and I were living together and he was helping with the bills. I told God, "I can't right now, how am I going to pay the bills without him?" I was no stranger to the word; I knew that I would have to give the boyfriend up to follow Jesus. Then I heard God say, "Trust me." God don't force us to love Him, his mercy endures forever, and He patiently waited for me. (Thank you God) Eventually, a few months later, I left the relationship and asked God, "Now what?" Again I heard "Trust me." I would love to say I trusted Him and we lived happily ever after. I began to go to church and study the word more, but I constantly worried about the finances. I got a second job but worked so much and was so tired that I couldn't enjoy the fruits of my labor and only had enough to make ends meet.

God eventually allowed me to get fired, because I wasn't going to quit. The day I got fired I remember God saying trust me over and over in my spirit. This time I did trust Him. I didn't try to find another job, gave up premarital sex and began living a life of holiness for the Lord. Then one year passed then two years and no relationship. Now I am asking God, how long must I wait. I desired marriage. As Christians we feel that if we live holy then God owes us and our desires will be answered quickly. Wrong! Remember God is a God of order, everything is in His timing.

Have you ever stopped to think that you are not ready? Yep I said it, you are not ready. This was a painful realization for me too. While working the second job, I was new to the Christian walk and needed some gospel music. I had a few CDs but needed something new and up to date. A friend at my day job gave me a Jessica McClendon CD. While listening to "Who can love you better", it finally hit me. It wasn't that God didn't want me to get married; He wanted me to learn to love Him and myself. I was lonely and depressed, questioning God every day.

Sin pulls you away from God, in order for Him to send you that husband or wife He must get rid of your old sinful ways. In order to do that you must spend time with Him, developing a personal relationship. God is a jealous God. He is not going to allow anyone to come into your life that is going to take His place. If we are absolutely honest, we know that the minute we get a boyfriend or girlfriend the first thing to suffer is our relationship with Christ.

We must give Him complete control over every aspect in our lives. Complete control requires absolute trust. Do you really trust God? Or do you put Him in a box only allowing him control when you have exhausted all possibilities. Don't feel ashamed I had this same problem. We are unable to trust God because everyone we trusted in the past let us down. I had been hurt so many times by so many men that I saw God just like man: Conditional love, loving me as long as I was giving up something. I just could not believe that I could do nothing to deserve or keep His love. When I messed up, I felt He was angry at me or would punish me. I also felt that because of the sin of my past I was undeserving of His love and blessings. But this is exactly what the devil wants you to believe. When we think like this it pushes us further and further from God.

God does not walk away from us; we (through sin) walk away from him. The devil uses memories from the past to drive us further away. But as my pastor says, "Aren't you glad we serve a God of second chances?" The bible says He will never leave you nor forsake you. God is waiting for you with open arms. Are you ready to receive Him? But the key again is trust. To trust God, you have to know that He knows what's best for you and will not lead you astray.

Trust in the Lord with all your heart, and lean not on your own understanding; in all your ways acknowledge Him and He shall direct your paths. - Proverbs 3: 5 – 6

To trust God means to 1. Let go of the past and 2. Give Him control of the present and future. God understands this is not easy. This is why He gives us tests and rewards along the way. If you remember how He brought you out of the small things then it will build your faith to trust Him in the big things. Nothing pleases the Father more than to bless his children. He knows you want to be married, but there are some things in you that must come out first. You didn't think that once you got saved then everything would be A OK, did you? If we tell the truth, most of us have been sinners longer than we have been saved. Especially since we are all born sinners (sin natured). Therefore God has to get all that junk out and reprogram you before He brings someone else into your life.

Until then your focus should be on God and the things of God.

Stop focusing on what you don't have

As I said earlier, not only is God trying to bless you in other areas, He requires our praise as well. Praise Him for what He has already done.

I remember you, the kindness of your youth, the love of your betrothal, when you went after Me in the wilderness, in a land not sown. - Jeremiah 2: 2b

Israel had forgotten what the Lord had done for them bringing them out of bondage and began to slip back into their old ways. This is what we do to the Lord when we begin to murmur and complain about what we don't have. Remember how you felt when you first got saved or first repented and decided to follow Jesus. I do. I couldn't get enough of my Father. I was at church every time the doors opened. Tuesday morning prayer, Wednesday night bible study, Sunday morning prayer, Sunday school, Sunday morning worship and Sunday night worship. Usually I was one of the first ones there. I read my bible every day and God was talking to me every day all day. I was so excited I would share what He told me with others. Though they would look at me like "what does that got to do with me," I didn't care. We were building a relationship;

He was showing me His love for me. But I let my desire for a relationship overshadow all that.

The world is in the middle of a recession. I still have a full-time job, my own house, own car, food on the table and clothes on my back, yet I am depressed about not having a man! How is it we can have everything we need yet focus on the one thing we want and feel deprived or forsaken? Imagine how God feels, we must seem like ungrateful spoiled brats. Part of praising God is recognizing and giving thanks for all He has done. When praises go up, blessings come down. When we praise and thank God for the things we have we impel Him to give us more.

The Lord does not come to our pity parties. Complaining prevents us from hearing from God and it prolongs our forward progress. You can't go anywhere standing still. God has such big plans for us. Marriage is one of many. Writing this book is one of God's plans for me. I talked myself out of it before I even started. God gave me the title and the names of eight chapters. I researched on the internet: how to write a book, self-publishing, standard length of a chapter and so forth, never really finding a concrete answer. Then I looked at books from some of my favorite authors like Joyce Myers and TD Jakes, looked at their writing style and length of chapters. Again nothing concrete, because all writers have a different style. So finally I told myself that a chapter should be 15 to 20 pages long. With 8 chapters the book should be about 120 to 160 pages. Oh my God, how am I going to write all that, when am I going to find the time? Two weeks past, two months past, and then a whole year, still nothing accomplished. No book, yet I'm still looking for my husband. How can I want something from God and I can't do what He asked. One day I heard the Holy Ghost say 'Just write". So one night I sat down and in a matter of two hours I had typed 5 pages 7 if you count the title page and table of contents. It just flowed. Then I got busy again, and more months past. I shared my desire to write a book with a co-worker, he offered to read it and let me know what he thought. He stated it was good but too preachy. I said all this to say. Don't let anyone including yourself prevent you from being all that God wants you to be. So what if He doesn't give you what you want in the order you think you should have it.

But seek ye first the kingdom of God and His righteousness and all these things shall be added to you. - Matthew 6:33

We all have a purpose; we must walk in that purpose whether we have a spouse right now or not. If you focus on what you don't have, you can't be grateful for what you do have and you will miss what you could have. Then years later you will be singing your could a, would a, should a's basking in regret.

Stop living in the past

You can't move forward looking back; you'll trip and fall over what's in front of you. Remember in the book of Genesis, when God told Lot to get his family and leave Sodom and Gomorrah because He was about to destroy it. They were told not to look back, but Lot's wife looked back and turned into a pillar of salt. Looking back literally killed her. Once God has forgiven us and provided a way of escape, why go back? Why reminisce on the pain and the heartache? The sins of the past are over and done and have no bearing on the future. The past is what got us here in the first place. The devil replays events of our past and allows us to remember vividly how good it felt to be indulged in that sin. We can remember exact feelings and smells.

Why do you think it is so hard to do right? Because the flesh remembers how easy it was and how good it felt to do wrong. Sin is what kept you from God, why would He want you to go back to something that caused separation. God forgives and throws your sin into the sea of forgetfulness. He does not hold it against you. The devil wants you to stay. Why? Because it leads to feeling unworthy: unworthy of God's love, unworthy of God's mercy and unworthy of God's grace. Thus forgetting who you are and whose you are.

Don't get me wrong, the past has its' purpose. You are not supposed to forget where you came from or what God has delivered you from. Its purpose is to serve as a testimony to others struggling with the same problem or similar situation. It is also faith building. If God helped you then He will certainly help you now and tomorrow. It is also confidence building. It is one thing to see what God is doing for someone else and rejoice, but to see Him move in your own life is amazing. There is nothing like knowing God for yourself!

Again, trials and tribulations are part of the Christian walk. Trials strengthen us and help God prepare us for our destiny. Some trials are self-imposed, because we try to do things our way, get in over our head and have to suffer the consequences. Others are God-ordained to test our faith. If we could only get it in our head, the devil does not have the power to control life and death. I say this because I get sick of hearing testimonies that begin "the devil tried to kill me but God saved me!" Not to take light of anyone's suffering, but the devil can't do anything to you without God's permission (assuming you belong to God).

Remember in the book of Job. Job 1: 1-12 tells how righteous Job was, his many possessions, and how he loved and served the Lord with his whole heart. God basically asked

Satan "have you considered my servant Job?" Satan proclaimed that God protected him and all that he had but if it were taken away that Job would surely curse Him. God granted Satan permission to go after Job, telling him to do as he pleased "only do not lay a hand on his person." We give the devil too much credit. We blame him for our down falls, regrets and past mistakes. When truth is we did it because it felt good doing it. I believe we hold on to the past because we have yet to learn the lesson in the suffering and thus trying to figure God out.

Society wants us to believe that a merciful and gracious God does not allow bad things to happen. They look for explanations for child molestation, rape, murder, earthquakes, floods, or any violent crimes against children or innocent and 'good' people. God is God, it is impossible to figure out why he allows things to happen. It is not our job to figure out why he does what he does but it is our job to obey his word. In my personal opinion, God said "all have sinned and come short of his glory and that the wages of sin is death." He promised all will die, He never said it was going to be silently in our sleep or at a particular age.

Instead of questioning His motives we should instead ask: God what is it you want me to learn from this? How will this be used for your glory? Don't get me wrong this is a difficult task. I was molested five times before my thirteenth birthday.

Indiana Tuggle

A molested child grows up thinking adults are out to hurt them and are unable to protect them. I grew up angry at my mother because she was unable to protect me and did not get me any help. There was and still is a lot of resentment there, but God is helping me through it. I could not imagine anything good coming out of such a hurtful situation. After all it wasn't my fault, I didn't do anything wrong. When I find myself dwelling on it, I often tell myself: it wasn't that bad, you were only touched, get over it, let it go, move on, or other people and/or children have been through far worse. This is also a trick of the enemy. The devil wants you to believe that your feelings are unwarranted or unimportant. But God is concerned about everything about you. If it's important to you, it's important to God. Perhaps I should be over it; nevertheless the effect it had on my life requires healing only God can give.

I said all this to say, give the past to God. If you need deliverance allow Him to deliver. If you need healing allow Him to heal. God does not want us to dwell on the hurt He wants us to live victorious.

Do not remember the former things, nor consider the things of old. Behold, I will do a new thing, now it shall spring forth; shall you not know it? I will even make a road in the wilderness and rivers in the desert. - Isaiah 43: 18-19

I love this passage. God is trying to take us to our destiny and we are stuck in the past. He proclaims, (even if we don't fully understand where we are going and may get lost along the way), he will give us a way of escape and rejuvenate the dry places. In other words He will give you the strength to get back up and start again. God loves to keep blessing His children. If He delivered you once He can definitely do it again. Miracles are not just a myth; God did not just speak to Moses, David, Abraham, Isaac, and Jacob. He is stilling doing miracles and giving us direction today. All He asks is that we allow Him to take the wheel and trust that He knows the way.

Let Go and Let God

Letting go and letting God expounds on being able to trust God. As Christians we often want to believe we are allowing God control of our lives. But let's just take a moment to examine ourselves a little deeper. To let go and let God is more than a cliché and is harder than it seems. As singles this is even harder, especially if you have been single, or shall I say without a relationship, for five or more years. We are used to doing things for ourselves, when we want to and how we want to. Do we really know how to wait and allow someone else to do things for us? Not just someone else, God!

Indiana Tuggle

It makes God happy to bless his children yet we tie His hands by trying to help Him out. Take Sarah and Abraham for example. God told Sarah He would give her a child out of her own womb. Instead of rejoicing in the promise and patiently waiting for its fruition, she first laughed at the impossible and second decided to take matters into her own hand by having Abraham go in to her maid, Hagar. Every time we jump ahead of God and try to make things happen for ourselves we too are laughing at God. What we are saying is, I hear you but it will be impossible unless I do something. Or because it is not happening fast enough, God must want me to intervene. We must not confuse the scripture "faith without works is dead" with impatience, lack of discipline and lack of trust.

For the vision is yet for an appointed time; but at the end it will speak, and it will not lie. Though it tarries, wait for it; because it will surely come, it will not tarry. - Habakkuk 2:3

If God said it we can take it to the bank! God is not a liar. Everything He said concerning you will come to pass, in His own perfect timing. We can't continue to treat God like the men or women who hurt us, full of broken promises.

I too said, not me, I trust God with everything. That's what I was saying when I went out and got the second job. There is nothing wrong with people working a second job, but it is not a justification for being disobedient. God clearly said trust him. He is my provider; He will supply all my needs. It was not until I "coincidently" got fired that I trusted God. But what about when the bills are due and you have to make a decision to pay your tithes or your bills, or when the doctor calls you in for more testing. Financial troubles and sickness will quickly reveal who has your trust. Trials come our way to build our faith.

As singles we tend to put our faith in our own abilities. We adapt the "I can do it myself" attitude. Letting go and letting God requires relationship with God. How can you know His character and His promises for you if you don't spend time with Him? Reading the word, praying, fasting, and meditating are essential to building that relationship. The more you spend time with Him the more you can turn things over to Him because you know He can and will do it for you. Start with the small things. If He blesses you in the small areas the quicker you are to turn over the big things. We easily grasp this concept with man but are slow to apply it with God. You don't meet someone today and give them the keys to your house tomorrow. You spend time with them and get to know them. Why do we have so much patience with man, yet expect to move so quickly with God? Yes He knows us better than we know ourselves but do we know Him? To really know Him is to wait patiently with expectation of the things to come, knowing that no matter when it arrives it will be right on time!

Indiana Tuggle

Chapter 2

If I Don't Get Him/Her, I Will Still Praise Him

You changed my sorrow into dancing. You took away my clothes of sadness, and clothed me in happiness. I will sing to You and not be silent. Lord my God, I will praise You forever.
Psalm 30: 11 – 12

I am learning the secret to contentment. It's in the praise, this is one of many reasons why I love the book of Psalms. David was a man after God's own heart. Through Psalm, through praise, he showed us how to get close to God. If you ever wanted or needed anything from God, it begins with praise. Praise is so important because it takes focus off of self and redirects it to the One who can do all things. Praise signifies gratitude and expectancy. Gratefulness for what He has already done and expectancy of what He has promised to be done. When you praise God, He has no choice but to move on your behalf.

Praise does not just ignite God to give you what you want. It is to help you be happy with what you have, acknowledging that even though He may not have given you everything you want, He has provided all you need. God does not want us to take Him and His blessings for granted. There is always, always a reason to give Him praise.

Praise breaks down the barricade to your heart and reveals the real you. It builds integrity. It keeps you in tune to the things of God and heaven. Praise opens your spiritual eyes and enables you to see things through the eyes of God. Praise brings about a positive attitude, which is impossible to the natural eye. The natural eye only sees what is going on or happening now, while the spiritual eye sees what is to come. The way you see things determines your verbal connotation towards them. Every word we speak takes root and brings forth fruit whether positive or negative. If you speak positive words, positive things will happen and if you speak negative words, negative things will happen. So if praise is so important, and God requires our praise, then why is it so difficult for believers to give God what He deserves?

Cut the enemy off at the knees

It's time to take back what the devil stole. In order to come against the enemy you must begin to shut down his power. We know that God is patient, but we forget that Satan is patient too. God created us with a purpose before He formed us in the wound (Jeremiah 1:5). The devil may not know your future but he knows your past. His job is to throw everything in his power at you to keep you from the truth. Every word he has whispered in your ear, you must snatch it out at the root. One night at bible study we did an exercise. We were instructed to write down every negative word that we could think of that had been spoken over us. I remember writing: Nobody loves you, You're fat, You're black and ugly, You're stupid, You can't do that, You are better off dead, Nobody will miss you, and You're all alone. Then we were instructed to get out a red pen and cross every statement out that we had written down. The red pen represented the blood of Jesus. The blood cancels out every idle word the devil has spoken over your life.

For every negative word the devil has spoken over your life, begin to replace it with the word of God:

The Devil Says	The Bible Says
Nobody loves you	God loves me because He sent Jesus to die for me. (John 3:16)
You're fat, black and ugly	I am fearfully and wonderfully made in God's own image. (Psalm 139:14-16; 1 Tim 4:4)
You're stupid, you can't do that	I can do all things through Christ who strengthens me (Phil 4:13)
You're better off dead	I come to give you life and life more abundantly. (John 10:10)
You're all alone	I will never leave nor forsake you. (Deut 31:6; Heb 13:5-6)

If we fight the enemy with the word, he has to flee. That does not mean he won't come back. It means he will repackage it and present it to you another way. Relationship with God is absolutely essential for fighting off the enemy. Relationship means studying and reading the word, praying, fasting, and meditating. The more we build our relationship with God the more ammunition we have to fight. When we are low on ammunition, the tricks of the enemy leads us to depression, frustration, confusion, anger, bitterness, etc., all of which pushes us further from God and hinders us from giving Him praise.

Recognize what hinders your praise

Which of you by worrying can add one cubit to his stature? - Matthew 6:27

Worrying is one of the biggest hindrances to our praise. We become so overwhelmed by the stresses at work, home, school etc. On a day to day basis my thoughts are consumed with thoughts about finances, how can I do this, how can I do that and my need for a better paying job or a career in the field in which I obtained the degree. The problem with worrying is we generally are concerned about things we have no control over.

I see the serenity prayer everywhere: at people's houses, in doctor's offices, in cubicles at work, etc. But do we actually believe and practice what it says? The bible says we have not because we ask not. So the only thing we can control is the asking. We are to make our requests known to God and believe that He will grant our desire. We cannot control the when, where and how. God decides when we will get it, where we will get it, and how it will come to pass. We worry because when we made the request we were expecting it right then. We even go so far as to explain why we deserve it: I pay my tithes, I work hard in the church, I live right, I help others, etc. We can't fathom that God's timing is not our timing. As my pastor says God is time, 20 years to us may be just one day to him. We can never "do" enough to "deserve" a specific blessing. If God's blessing were based on merit, if we are honest, we would never get anything because we are not perfect. God controls the timing, if what He promised has not come to pass, you will not die before it does! In our impatience we even try to help God out by trying to fix the situation ourselves, more often than not, this creates a bigger hole to get out of.

When we feel God has not given us something we think we deserve, we cannot praise him for the things he has given us. We become frustrated and angry which leads to a strain on our relationship with God. We stop studying and praying, which opens a window for the enemy to come in. We have to understand God's delay is not a denial. God does not make us wait just for the sake of waiting. The waiting is for us not Him. We wait because we are not ready, to increase our faith, and because there is a lesson in the waiting. Trials test our faith; there may be something in you, some negative attribute that God needs to deliver you from before He takes you to that next level. Realizing I was not ready for marriage was one of the hardest things I had to deal with. Mainly because it was something I desired so badly. But when God pointed out my character flaws, like anger, bitterness, and low self-esteem, I could not see bringing a man into that type of situation. I would scare the man off with my attitude. But I wanted a healthy, long-lasting marriage more than just having one for the sake of having one. Now I see the revelation was easy, it's the deliverance that's going to be hard.

A merry heart makes a cheerful countenance, but by sorrow of the heart the spirit is broken. - Proverbs: 15:13

Unhappiness also hinders our praise. If we are not happy with ourselves or happy with our present lives it's impossible to praise God. Unhappiness leads to continual dissatisfaction. An unhappy person is very pessimistic, unable to see the bright side of things. They feel if they can't or don't do something things will not get better. And in all their trying, it just seems things still don't turn around. It's because we are trying to be God! Don't get me wrong there are some things that God has promised that require action on our part. The bible says "faith without works is dead," as well as "the steps of a good man are ordered by the Lord." So before we spring into action we need direction from God. Unhappiness comes from doing things on our own and not getting the results we wanted. There are also things in our life that happen that steal our joy.

    I can remember times in my life when I was a happy go lucky person, always smiling, and always laughing. Unfortunately those times disappeared in my adult life. I asked God what happened to my joy. He took me down a trip through memory lane and I saw when and where the joy started to disappear. I have been overweight most of my life and as a child obesity is difficult to deal with. Children can be very cruel. I could not deal with the taunting. At first I became a bully, fighting everybody who had something negative to say. But my parents would often spank me for fighting, so I had no other defense mechanism. If I taunted back, it just didn't seem like I could do enough to stop the fat jokes. Whoever said "sticks and stones can break my bones but words will never hurt me," I need to find them and choke them, because obviously they never grew up fat. So I started to go in to myself, I became the quiet smart one. I definitely wasn't going to be fat and dumb. If I couldn't win the admiration of my classmates, I would win the admiration of my teachers by being the smartest one in the class. And that is what I did. I finished my work fast, helped the teachers with assignments, and scored the highest on aptitude tests. At home I would watch TV or play with dolls by myself and write letters to God in my diary about how I really felt.

In high school it seemed the taunting intensified, with so many students, teachers were not impressed by my intelligence and could no longer shield me from the taunting. Students no longer talked behind my back or pointed and laughed, they were bold enough to say it directly to my face. So I began searching for love and acceptance. But I never really fit in. One night when I was twelve years old, while babysitting my younger cousin, my aunt & her boyfriend came in late after a night of partying. My cousins and I were sleeping in the living room, some on the floor and my baby cousin and I on the couch, she lying on my chest. The boyfriend came in to get my cousin off me and grabbed a feel of my breasts while doing so. My brother was there so I woke him and told him what happened and we walked in the dark down the street to the pay phone to call my mom. I remember my mom telling me, he didn't mean it, you're a big girl your breast are mostly fat anyway.

At thirteen, at a cousin's slumber party it happened again. This time my cousin and I were sleep in her bed upstairs. Her father came in, after a night of partying, crawled into the room on his knees and put his hands in my underwear. I woke in a cold sweat and ran home to tell my mom. We discovered that before he came upstairs to me, he stopped and did the same thing to my other cousin who was sleeping downstairs. The police were called and we had to go to the rape crisis center. The technician who did the examination testified in court that the man had pressed against my genitals so hard you could see his finger prints. The guy was sentenced to seven years in jail. I never received psychiatric treatment and was left feeling that my innocence was stolen. So I began to give it away, stating I'd rather give it away than to have it taken.

Each situation played a part in the unhappy person I am today. When I can't express myself I get angry and take out my frustrations on others around me. If Satan can get you to be quiet, bottle everything inside, he can keep you from becoming the person God wants you to be.

I said, "I will guard my ways, lest I sin with my tongue; I will restrain my mouth with a muzzle, while the wicked are before me." I was mute with silence, I held my peace even from good; and my sorrow was stirred up. My heart was hot within me; while I was musing, the fire burned. Then I spoke with my tongue: - Psalm 39:1-3

Until reading this passage, I did not understand the importance of silence to the enemy. Silence was my natural reaction when I felt unheard or misunderstood. By being silent, I thought I was protecting myself from being hurt again, but I was actually totally disregarding my feelings. Silence also makes us frustrated. Though your thoughts are not outwardly projected, they are inwardly corroding the spirit. On the inside you ponder things over and over in your mind, and because there is no outward flow, they go in circles leading to nowhere and no decision being made. Indecisiveness also leads to frustration and confusion. The longer you are silent the more you regret not being outspoken and you dwell on what should have been said. Then one day you explode and a surplus of mixed emotions comes out and you become angry and bitter.

A confused Christian is double-minded and unstable. If Satan can keep you in this state, you can't move forward, you can't recognize and act on Gods voice. God's voice gets scrambled in among all the other thoughts, thus leading to doubt and unbelief. When we doubt God the spirit of fear easily finds entrance into our hearts. Fear keeps you from relying on the strength of God and focusing on your own shortcomings. You question Gods purpose and are hesitant to give him control. If God does not have control, how can we find reason to praise him? It's in our praise that we realize his absolute power and control over everything. He has control over yesterday, today, and tomorrow. Praise breaks the silence.

The dead do not praise the Lord, nor any who go down in silence. - Psalm 115:17

God created us to praise him. By keeping silent we refuse to give God what he deserves and thus are in direct disobedience. Silence leads to passiveness. Christians are not pushovers. We are to be steadfast, unmovable and always standing firm on the word of God. The bible warns us to choose our words carefully and not to boast or brag, but that does not mean to stand by and allow evilness to prevail. Silence does not speak to good or evil, therefore by default evil triumphs.

Praise leads to worship

As I stated earlier, praise thanks God for what He has done or will do in the future. Praise expresses our gratitude. Worship expresses adoration and reverences His power. Praise without worship is empty lip service or going through the motion.

I could never understand why during church service, I could not connect with God. The service would be high and others would be crying out, dancing, or speaking in tongues. Yet I would just observe wondering why I could not have my God moment. Yelling out an occasional "thank you, Lord" or "hallelujah" was not getting it. I knew the right words but there were no feelings behind it. I was merely saying them out of tradition or repetition. Now I understand. Worship does not start on Sunday. Worship is our lifestyle. We must worship Him daily by spending time with Him, praying, meditating, reading and studying the word. Then we apply what we learned on the job, at school, at practice, at church, or basically everywhere our normal routine takes us. We worship God by living a life of holiness. We cannot express our love for God more than living according to his commandments and allowing Him complete control of our daily lives. If we wait till Sunday, we will be weighted down with the cares of the world looking for the preacher to make us feel better.

True worship begins by acknowledging and realizing we are nothing without God. Worship is a time for the spirit man to connect with God. I will never forget, October 10, 2010 it was the day I was filled with the Holy Spirit with the evidence of speaking in tongues. It was the most amazing feeling. At that exact moment God became real to me. It was like at that moment I knew God was with me all along. In the month before this day, I had two break-ins at my home about a month apart. The first time they stole a TV, a laptop, and a cell phone, but I was financially unable to get the repairs done and was waiting on someone to give me an estimate for the insurance company. Exactly 30 days later I had another break-in, through the same window, but the alarm went off and though they stole nothing, they damaged the electricity meter trying to make the alarm go off. And no the alarm was not on the first time. Actually it wasn't on the second time; it was just a noise maker, since I hadn't paid the bill. I tried to be a big girl about the situation; I was quiet as usual, acting as if I wasn't bothered in public. But truth is I was scared to death. I would come home every day checking windows, closets, and doors for signs of forced entry or someone hiding. I couldn't sleep, I would stay up all night usually only getting about 2 hours of sleep. I had panic attacks and dizzy spells. Did I pray? I tried a little but not as much as I should have been. Honestly I didn't know what to say, I was literally speechless. I thought by trying to hold it together I was being strong and going through with grace. In actuality, I had given up the fight. The filling of the Holy Ghost was my ammunition to fight. Before that day I was literally fighting speaking in tongues. I didn't understand what it meant and why I needed it. In my eyes, I already had Jesus; He communed with me all the time. But now I understand that speaking in tongues allows my spirit man to commune with God in the spirit. The bible says "They that worship him must worship Him in spirit and truth." Speaking in tongues is our heavenly language and cannot be understood by the devil. If the devil doesn't know what you are saying he cannot come against it. Even when in the flesh we are at a loss for words, the spirit man always knows what to say.

True worship is a time to ask for nothing (materially) but to be in His presence. It's a time to just love on Him just because of who He is to you. That's one of many things I love about God. He is many different things to each of us but is the same for all of us. Through our trials and tribulations God reveals another aspect of His personality. Through the bible and the testimony of others we learn what God can and will do for us. But when He does it for you personally, the story goes from what you heard to what you know. Through my financial situations God became my provider, through my home invasion God became my comforter and present help. When we worship God, it becomes real from our personal relationship with Him. If you have no relationship with Him and cannot grasp the things that He has kept you from then you will be unable to truly worship Him.

True worship also requires us to focus on God! This is a difficult task. Too many believers are weighted down by the cares of the world and selfish ambition. Either things are going bad and we are too lost to find God or things are going too good and we fill we don't need God. We are worrying too much about tomorrow. Only God can see tomorrow. Whether times are good or bad, or whether the devil is fighting you or not, the devil does not know your future and cannot see your tomorrow. God knows our present and future, it's already planned. We prolong tomorrow's blessing by focusing on what we are missing today, thus not acknowledging the many things and reasons we have to worship God. He deserves our praise and worship whether we have what we want or not. When we can praise God even when things don't look too good we have crossed into true worship. True worship acknowledges that we may not fully understand our present trials but we trust that God will work it out for our good and His glory.

Ungratefulness is a big hindrance to worship and giving God praise. Most feel it is impossible to be a Christian and be ungrateful at the same time. Which is true, but I don't think Christians realize they are ungrateful (not giving due return or recompense for benefits conferred). I am a big fan of gospel music however I am also a lyric person meaning I pay close attention to the words of a song and analyze every word and try it against the word. One song in particular comes to mind. I don't know the title, but the chorus says "He may not come when you want Him, but He'll be there right on time, He's and on time God, Yes He is!" I don't claim to know everything, but how can someone be on time yet not there when you want them? That would imply that he/she is late or you were just impatient. Indicating God does not come when you want Him implies that we set the time. As we mature in Christ, we learn time belongs to God and God is time. God wants to bless us but He has to condition us to receive it. Worship helps us through the wait period. God is never late and He is never early. The wait period was designed to flush out impurities that will keep us from the blessings of God. Ungratefulness is one of those impurities.

For the invisible things of him from the creation of the world are clearly seen, being understood by the things that are made, even his eternal power and Godhead; so that they are without excuse: Because that, when they knew God, they glorified him not as God, neither were thankful; but became vain in their imaginations, and their foolish heart was darkened.
- Romans 1: 20-21

The bible teaches us that every good perfect gift comes from God; however Job 14:1 proclaims that "man that is born of woman is of few days and full of trouble". So we can see that even the bad days are ordered by the Lord. It is hard to worship God when you are unable to see the bright side of every situation. The devil cannot do anything in this earth without God's permission. We've all heard the saying, "the devil meant it for evil but God meant it for good". When you can't praise God through the trouble you are in turn giving the devil glory. Lacking praise or thankfulness prohibits God to move in your life. It took me some time to realize this. Ungratefulness was the reason behind my empty praises. My prayer to God was for Him to allow me to see His power in my life.

When I was a child, I was basically a loner. I was overweight so I didn't have many friends. Kids at school were so cruel and I got teased every day. When I got home I would retreat to my room with snacks and play on the floor with my Barbie dolls and doll house made of milk crates. (the real one was too expensive). At the end of each day I would write in my diary telling God about my day and how I felt. By the time I reached 4th grade, I was so angry at the teasing I became a bully and starting fighting the kids who teased me. By high school I was tired of fighting and just started keeping my feelings bottled up. Trying to fit in I hung out with the wrong crowds and got into skipping school, marijuana, and premarital sex. In high school my mom was pretty strict not allowing me to hang out or even date. At 13 I was molested by the boyfriend of my cousin's mother. So by 14 it was really no surprise that I started having sex. I was with the same guy throughout high school. My need for love and attention caused me to put up with his infidelity.

My adult years were followed with one bad relationship after the next. Not to mention the man I knew as my father was very abusive to my mother. I remember on several occasions hearing her screaming for help or hearing her body hit the wall. One night, I think I was 12 or 13, I was sleeping and about 3am my mother came running into my room, screaming and jumped into my bed. As I awakened, heart pounding with fear, my father came running in behind her with a hammer in his hand. He grabbed her by her hair and started beating her in her head with the hammer. She and I both were screaming. He then grabbed her by the head and started ramming her head into the turning fan that I had in the window. By now I jumped up, ran out the house to my aunt's house who lived down the street and called the police. I don't remember if he went to jail that night or not. My brother was a few years older than me so most of the fights happened when he was out with friends.

I took a trip down memory lane to show, that I experienced a lot of hurt and heart ache in my young life. I am just realizing that through it all God was still there. He has always been my shield and protector. I never understood why my mother was so strict on me or why I never fit in though I tried so hard. It was because God was protecting me from a destructive path. My mother knew the path I was going, as she traveled the same, and she was trying to protect me as well. I was lonely, depressed and looking for love, but God protected me from the wrong influences and didn't let me drown in my sin. I was promiscuous and thought I was behaving like an adult, but God shielded me from STDs, Aids, and unwanted/unplanned pregnancies. Though I was molested, God shielded me from rape. Though my house was broken into, God shielded me from death. I have had a lot of trials and tribulations and through it all God allowed me to keep my right mind, go through school, get multiple degrees, and most importantly He made me strong enough to bear it and testify of His goodness to others. Why? He had a plan and a purpose.

Overcoming the hurts and pains of the past is difficult, but God promises not to put more on us than we can bare. We must allow God to work in us. I went through the last couple of years throwing a pity party. Thinking my past was too heavy to walk away from yet not that bad to continue to allow it to hold me down. I realized that I was treating God, just like another man in my life who let me down and filled me with empty promises leaving me feeling worthless, unimportant and unworthy. But God is not a man that He should lie and He promised never to leave nor forsake me. He promised to be my God, if I let him!

Chapter 3

He That Findeth

He who finds a wife finds a good thing, and obtains favor from the Lord.
Proverbs 18:22

The key word in the scripture is "finds". Most use this verse as an excuse to search for a mate. I will visit the searching part later. But when I think of the word find, what immediately comes to mind is something or someone is lost. Or something or someone is not visible to the seeker or is hidden. Let's go back to the beginning when God made Adam.

And the Lord God said, "It is not good that man should be alone; I will make him a helper comparable to him. - Genesis 2: 18

What I like about this scripture is God, not Adam, said that it was not good for Adam to be alone. Therefore Adam was not looking for a wife. God decided he needed one, and not just anyone, one comparable to him, so he formed Eve from Adam's rib. God presented Eve to Adam when He decided the time was right. God sees all and knows all; He has hidden that mate, whom is comparable to us, until the appropriate time. If God has hidden something, you can rest assured it will stay hidden until He is ready to reveal it. So in essence, "to find a wife" means to see with the natural eye whom God has set aside for you and what was once hidden has been made not only visible but also available to you.

I have been celibate for a little over 5 years now. After the first few years, I became disgruntle not understanding why I had not found my husband. It has been prophesied that I would get married. I have even dreamed of my wedding and my husband, only his face was blurry or not revealed. I'm curious by nature. I even tried to help God out by online dating. I don't have to mention the trouble this can lead to. I will say this though, just because you are honest doesn't mean the other person is also honest. Also a picture or brief description does not disclose true intentions. I finally accepted that my time has not come. So I asked God, why? He said I was not ready. That took some days to take in. You mean after years of living according to the word and waiting for Mr. Right, I am not ready? Deep breathe…So I asked, "Why am I not ready?" He answered: "Before you can love anybody else you must first love yourself. No one can love you better than you. If you can't love yourself, how can you understand my love for you?"

Start with God

Learning to love begins with the creator. To love ourselves means to love ourselves unconditionally. Regardless of the character flaws, non-perfect bodies, past hurts, mistakes, lack of education, lack of wealth, or whatever the devil has used to make you feel unworthy, we must first understand we are capable of being loved. All these things whether limited or in abundance contribute to the person we are or are going to be. God is love. Because of His love He created us in His own image, and everything He made was good and perfect. Because of His love He sent Jesus to show us how to live and care for others and bear our sins upon the cross. There is no greater love than the love of Jesus.

He who does not love does not know God, for God is love. - 1 John 4:8

If we are lacking love it is because we do not understand who God is and the depth of his love for us. How do we get to know God? Everything we need is in the word. John 1:1 states "in the beginning was the word, the word was with God, and the word was God." How can we expect to draw closer to God or learn who He is and how to trust Him without reading the word? Praying alone does not develop a well-rounded relationship with God. Without the word, prayers can be empty, full of random words, and/or materialistic requests. God does not go against His word; He cannot speak without the word. By not reading the word we limit God's communication with us to Sunday morning. By Sunday we are so bogged down by our own issues we can't really hear or are not paying attention or fully consuming what the preacher is saying.

Not reading the word leaves us vulnerable to the temptations of the devil and easily lead astray. Reading the word keeps us bright eyed and bushy tailed. We are receptive to what God is doing in our lives and our spiritual eyes are open to the devices of the enemy. Those who do not read the word for themselves flow to and fro with whatever or whomever tickles their ears during any period of time. If it sounds good and seems logical to their current situation, they will go with it.

The word enlightens us to God's purpose and plan for our lives. The word helps us see that everything that happened in our lives, good or bad, was ordained by God.

And the light shines in the darkness, and the darkness *did not comprehend it. - John 1:5*

God is the light in the darkness of our past. But because we do not comprehend (or understand) we do not allow Him to shine. The New Living translation states on the 2nd part of this verse "and the darkness can never extinguish it." No matter what has happened in the past, it does not eliminate or cancel the purpose and plan God has on our lives. We are to tell the world what He has done for us. It is difficult to comprehend how our hurts and sins of the past will be used for God's glory. But once we forgive ourselves, forgive those who hurt us, and accept God's forgiveness we can walk in victory. The past then becomes a tool to help others find Jesus and receive the same salvation and deliverance we have. I remember asking God "why me"? Why did I have to go through so many bad things? He responded "You were made to tell of My goodness. Once you realize who you are, you will be ready for My use. You are My child, born of Me. You are in My bosom, I have declared you righteous." Once God has thrown our sins into a sea of forgetfulness, the devil can no longer hold it over our head. Any power the devil has regarding our past is because we gave it to him.

The word adds sustenance to our prayers. Lack of the word makes us focus on worldly things. Day to day we spend too much time thinking about material possessions and financial hardships: what bill to pay, the money we need for clothes, shoes, food, repairs for the house and car. God knows what we need. The bible says "He will supply all our needs according to His riches in glory. (Philippians 4:19)" Psalm 34:10 also says "The young lions lack and suffer hunger; but those who seek the Lord shall not lack any good thing." We must focus on Gods needs and He will handle the rest. Our needs and wants are small pebbles in His hand. Our purpose is far greater than eyes can see. We learn to trust Him by focusing on His needs and He will focus on ours. The greatest thing God needs from us is our time. As we give our time He will give us direction and reveal the next steps. When you are frustrated, let go and give Him your time. When you are worried, give Him your time. Remember He is able to do exceedingly and abundantly above all you can ask or think. Trust that He knows what's best, be patient, and allow Him to complete a work in you.

Looking for love in all the wrong places

Simply put searching for love implies absence of love. Where there is no love there is no life. When searching for love we must ask ourselves why. Are we looking for someone to love or someone to love us? As Christians we should not be lacking in either. So if we find ourselves in a place in which we are lacking we must get to the root of the issue.

Many waters cannot quench love, nor can rivers drown it. - Song of Solomon 8:7a

Searching for love is rooted in a heart deemed unlovable. Rejection from a parent, abuse from friends or family, and broken hearts from past loves all spark a search for what appears to be missing. The problem is we are searching using faulty mechanisms. The bible tells us the heart is deceitful and wicked, therefore how can we use a deceitful wicked thing to find something pure belonging and coming from God? The pains and hurts of the past leave us with a false definition or expectation of what true unconditional love is. And send us on a journey to find something man cannot give. No man can make you love yourself! Only God can restore us and show us how to love and how to be loved.

Long ago the Lord said to Israel: "I have loved you, my people, with an everlasting love. With unfailing love I have drawn you to myself. I will rebuild you, my virgin Israel. You will again be happy and dance merrily with your tambourines." - Jeremiah 31:3-4

Our search for love is not for worldly love from man, it is a longing to be back in the grace and arms of the creator. But the heart has deceived us into thinking that what we desire is a man or woman. The enemy wants us to forget that God is the answer to everything, and everything we seek begins with God. Remember the story of the Samaritan woman whom Jesus met at the well? I love that story, each time I read it a different verse sticks out at me. John 4:4 says "But He needed to go through Samaria." God knew you needed Him before you knew Him. While you were searching for love, love was searching for you. You have felt like an outsider all your life unknowing that that which you have God can use for the kingdom. Your past is a witness to unbelievers of the grace of God. There is nothing you did, could do, or did not do that made you deserving or undeserving of God's love and grace. People will believe simply by your testimony, they will come to God and increase their faith.

Your past is a tool that led you to God. It is not the end of your journey. He is bigger than what you have seen and greater than what you can imagine. What awaits you is far bigger and better than what you came from. You have to think beyond yesterday. It is in the sea of forgetfulness. The love you seek is in Jesus. He is ready to give it you but you have to drink and if you do you will never thirst again. In return you will share this love with others.

Let go of the past

I have discovered that the key to letting go of the past is forgiveness. Forgiveness is hard to understand. We think that by forgiving we are condoning the abuse, the hurt, the pain, the suffering or better yet letting the accuser go with a slap on the wrist. I know we have heard it before but forgiveness is for you not the one who did the bad act. Why? Because if we don't forgive we give them the power to control our present.

I was watching a re-run of Oprah, and she quoted a statement from a past guest who said "Forgiveness is giving up the hope that the past could have been any different." This statement resonated deep into my soul and as the revelation took hold the tears began to flow. I finally understood true forgiveness. Forgiveness does not mean you forget the past or never discuss it. Forgiveness means you let go of the "what if, if this, if that, etc." No matter what we do, how long we think about it, dream about it, or how hard we wish, we cannot change the past. There are no do-overs. The second chance comes in using the past as empowerment to help someone else.

When Jesus saw him lying there, and knew that he already had been in that condition a long time, He said to him, "Do you want to be made well?" - John 5:6

We have to stop limiting God. Many see Him in one aspect, healer. Since you are not physically sick you don't acknowledge He can help or that help is even needed. You may not need healing but you do need deliverance. Though you have been carrying this for years, God knows and is able to deliver you, if you let Him. He can deliver you from the darkness to light, from the lie to the truth. He can rescue you from the lies of the past. He can rescue you from yourself. True deliverance is to remove you from the sin, remove you from the pain. How? By exposing the truth so that you may recognize the lie. Once the lie is made known you must dispel it with the truth. This does not mean the lie will never resurface. But each time it does, you must counter act it with the truth. Truth is in the word of God. The more you put the word into your mind and your heart, the further you get away from the lie and it can no longer be used to hinder you. Remember healing is for the body, deliverance is for the mind.

In that same Oprah re-run, Oprah was interviewing convicted child molesters and rapist. One of the rapist, made a very profound statement, when asked did he deserve to be in prison. He responded "Yes, in fact I am more than a rapist, I am a murderer; I killed who she would become." In that moment I recognized the enemy's plan. It was not about me and it is not about you. It is about stopping who God created you to be. My pastor once said "Satan's job, other than to steal, kill and destroy, is to embarrass God. You see Satan cannot control or stop our futures but he can hinder us by throwing obstacles in our way. The longer he keeps us from getting to what God wants us to do or has for us, he thinks he is embarrassing God. But unlike Satan God knows all, sees all, and is everywhere at all times. He knows that those obstacles will come and in fact allowed them to make us stronger and so He can use them for His glory. It is His love towards us that allows Him to patiently wait for us.

Seek after God not man

But seek ye first the kingdom of God and His righteousness, and all these things shall be added to you. - Matthew 6:33

The hardest thing for a Christian to hear, especially a baby saint, when they want something from God is "keep your eyes on God" or my personal favorite, "pray about it." Why is it so hard? Because it implies that we are not in control. And single folk, especially those over 30 don't ever want to admit they are not in control. I have learned that you won't get anything from God unless you relinquish control and truly trust him.

I mentioned earlier that God knows what we need and wants us to focus on His needs. In order for you to fully understand what God wants and has for you, it is imperative that you seek him diligently. The seeking is for you not God. He knows what's in you and what He needs to bring out of you. To seek God is to read and meditate on His word day and night, to pray daily and listen for His guidance and feedback, to welcome His chastisement and work hard daily to change those un-Christ like behaviors. And while we are seeking and waiting, we are to be patient and delight in knowing that what He has promised will come to past.

God knows we desire a spouse. He put that desire in us. But listen good and listen closely, God don't need your help! Trying to figure things out on your own is not patiently waiting on God. Online dating, going to the club with your friends in hopes of meeting someone special is not patiently waiting on God. Finding and looking for new hangouts, because you got to get out there to be seen, because Mr. or Mrs. Right is not going to knock on your door is not patiently waiting on God. Asking all your friends, who are in relationships, to hook you up with someone nice is not patiently waiting on God. Don't get me wrong, I'm not saying stay home and not have an active life, but getting involved in things solely for the purpose of meeting someone, will only open up the door for the devil to send Mr. /Ms. Wrong or Mr. /Ms. Right now.

Seeking God means to focus on the tasks He set before you. A mate is just one of God's many promises. Don't let not having one make you miss out on the joys of today. Remember the wait is for you, not God. If He promised you a mate, it will happen. But you have to believe that it will. Trying to find one on your own is a sign of unbelief. Faith without works is dead, but you can't do ALL the work. Let God be God and do what you can. Remove doubt from you heart. God is not a man that He should lie. Trust Him and don't get weary in well doing. Remember the word that was spoken over you; meditate on it with joyful expectation and watch God work.

What can you do during the wait? Continue to read the word and pray. Allow God to show you who you are and His desires and purpose for you. This road may not be smooth, in fact I can promise you it will be quite bumpy. But the ride will be worth it. Don't be afraid to ask questions. I had a dream a few months ago. In the dream I saw a man, a child, and a woman in a business suit standing and smiling behind what appeared to be a glass wall. They were blurred so I could not see their faces. I was on the other side, frustrated and frantically reaching for them. I could reach through the wall but I could not touch them. I took this dream to mean that my greatest desires, a husband, family, and career were in sight but I couldn't grasp them, something was blocking me. So I asked God, what is keeping me from those things. Fear, he replied.

I fear failure. I am afraid of messing up. What if I meet him, am swept off my feet, and give myself to him sexually ruining six years of celibacy and disappointing God? What if I get married and the relationship goes through hard times? What if I pick the wrong person? What if I get into the career and fail or better yet can't get a job? What if I am a bad mother and ruin my child for life? All of these what ifs signify one thing, unbelief. Failure is an option and it might happen, but success is also an option and it could happen. I have to have hope in the God in me and the Holy Spirit leading and guiding me, not in my own abilities. One thing is certain, I won't get anywhere if I don't try, step out on faith, and let God be God.

How can we be afraid of the very thing that we want so bad? Easily, it's the fear of the unknown. We can be so afraid of what will happen next, that we don't even do the first step. Hebrews tells us that faith is the substance of things hoped for and the evidence of things unseen. God is a God of order, he rarely reveals step two until step one is completed. He requires our faith.

Don't be afraid of sudden terror, nor of trouble from the wicked when it comes; for the Lord will be your confidence, and will keep your foot from being caught. - Proverbs 3:25-26

Fear makes the possible appear impossible. Fear keeps us stagnant. It's Satan's tool to delay the blessings God has for us. It frustrates us and causes us to question God. We have to remember fear did not come from God. It is not a feeling. We think that it is normal….perhaps. But it is a spirit and can only be fought by the word of God. This is another reason to continue to read the bible and pray. The word should give you the strength to face you fears. Fear comes when we try to do things in our own strength, which we will always fail. But when we call on the strength of the Lord we conquer fear and defeat the enemy.

We desire a Godly marriage. One that only God can give. We will never know what will happen tomorrow, but I do know that every day is a step closer to fulfilling my dreams and goals. I wouldn't chose not to wake up tomorrow if the choice were mine. Therefore if God blesses me to do so, why not ask,

"Since you gave me another day, what do you want me to do with it?"

Chapter 4

Delight Yourself in the Lord!

I will meditate on Your precepts, and contemplate Your ways. I will delight myself in Your statutes; I will not forget Your word.
Psalm 119: 15-16

In order for one to fully delight in the Lord, he/she has to be content with his/her present circumstances. Not just being ok with being single, but being ok with where you are in the Lord. You have to realize that you might not be where you want to be, but you are exactly where you need to be.

Relinquish your wants

I have already said a few times, you have to let go and let God. But this is imperative to your happiness and the key to getting what God has for you. Our wants for ourselves are just one line in the purpose and plan God has for us. We are unable to comprehend all God wants for us. So why then are we going to wallow in misery about one thing that we want and God has not provided yet? Why then are we going to let that one thing keep us from enjoying life and all the other things God is ready to give now?

Indiana Tuggle

We tend to write our wants down in an order of preference. I wanted to graduate college by 24, start my career by 25, then get married and have 2.5 kids and a dog by 30. Well I am three months shy of 35, working on my third degree, still haven't started on my dream job, no marriage and no kids. But when I think about it, whose time line was it, mine not God's? God does not operate on our timeline. Better yet did we even consult him on the desires or the timeframe? See our timeline is just a list of desires; it does not include the obstacles in the journey. My timeline didn't account for the boy crazy young adult who decided to move in with her boyfriend instead of going to college right after high school. Rather that starting college at 18 or 19, I started at 22. My timeline did not include the series of failed relationships, making it difficult for me to recognize Mr. Right if he slapped me in the face.

Our past may not hinder our future but it does slow us down and cause us to lose focus. We have to face reality, that when we come back to God, we have a lot of baggage that He has to deliver us from to get us back on track to becoming the man or woman of God He created us to be. But the beauty of trusting God and delighting in Him, is that there are rewards in the journey. Perhaps you can't have your husband or wife right now, but there are a plethora of things that are currently available. Just ask. True maturity is allowing God to order your steps.

With Christ life is just beginning

Life with God is a journey into the unknown. He is the driver and we are just passengers. We have to stop being side-seat drivers. We have to ask God to reveal his plan and be willing to be obedient to the tasks he sets before us. A few years back when I asked God what was I to be doing while waiting for my husband. He replied "living life to the fullest." My first task was to write this book. I realize now that, completing this book is not only my deliverance from the frustrations of being single but it is also the key to my joy. Writing has been a frustration release all my life. When I was a little girl I would write letters to God to vent my frustrations of being picked on at school and my true feelings that I was unable or afraid to express. It's something about putting my thoughts on paper that brings clarity and understanding.

This book is the key to understanding God's plan for me and being content with where I am in the journey. The Christian life is a continual process; the process is not over until death. Why wait for one thing to come to past to start enjoying it. As singles we have to let go of the "when I find a mate or when I get married," sentence. I have often said and frequently hear other singles talk about how they are going to go out more, try this and that, or travel more when they get married. If you are waiting until you get married to do things, then that means you are doing nothing now! What is stopping you now? Are we so afraid to do things on our own, that we would rather stay home miserable doing nothing? My 30th birthday was horrible. I was so depressed about not having anyone to take me out that I just went shopping and maxed out my credit card. I am still paying for that decision today. A week later I took myself to dinner and a movie. The movie was cool, once the lights go out; no one cares whether you are alone or not. Dinner was a little more difficult, because you feel like everyone is looking at you, especially if you have nothing to occupy your time while you wait. Now I understand why people bring a book or their laptop with them. It was a little awkward but I made it, and I really enjoyed myself.

If you don't enjoy spending time with yourself, what makes you think someone else will? Singleness is a time to discover who you are and what you like or dislike? If someone asks you what are your favorite things to do and you can't go beyond dinner and a movie, you are in big trouble. I was one of those who said I would travel more when I got married. But then God asked, why can't you travel now? Good question, what am I afraid of? Yes I would love to travel with my husband, but what is stopping me now. Well I am proud to say now, that I take two trips a year, sometimes more if I get the extra money. It's amazing the opportunities God will present to us if we just get out of our own way.

My next step is to find good clean fun in town. I often said I don't like crowds and I am not a club person. I am finding that it's not the crowd that bothers me. It's what the crowd is doing that I have a problem with. Hip hop music is not my thing, so I am very uncomfortable in clubs that focus on the rump shaking music. But a jazz spot with a live band and good food, I can definitely get down with that. I'm not a drinker so a bar or a place that pushes the drinking atmosphere will not appeal to me. The point is to discover what you like while you are single. I have seen unhappy married couples because one spouse got lost in the dreams and aspirations of the other at the expense of losing themselves. Marriage does not complete a person. You must already be complete before entering such a big commitment. I am not a marriage expert nor am I trying to be. Singleness is a time to focus on God and his plan for you. It's all about pleasing God, married folk have to worry about pleasing each other. But I do know that you can't please someone else if you are not happy with yourself.

Remember the word

It is the spirit who gives life; the flesh profits nothing. The words that I speak to you are spirit, and they are life. - John 6:63

Remember the word God has spoken over you. Remember the promises He made. We must follow God with expectation, constantly reminding Him of His promises. These expectations fuel our actions and keep our eyes on the prize. Nothing pleases God more than to repeat the word He has spoken back to Him. It almost forces Him to act on our behalf. Now that doesn't mean it will make Him give us something out of season. But it does show your willingness to wait on Him.

I have gotten several words about my husband. Rather than asking when Lord and complaining, I've learned to thank God for my husband and pray for him. I ask God to help him overcome the devices of the enemy and be the man God has called him to be. I also ask God to help me not to be anxious and patiently wait for His perfect timing. It's amazing how much peace you can get in praying for the mate you don't yet have. In addition if you can pray for him/her now, when you do meet and get married you won't have difficulty praying then. I certainly hope he is praying for me as well.

The words spoken over your life where not meant to bring pain and suffering or depression because they have not come to past. They are meant to bring life to a dead situation. They are meant to give joy for today and hope for tomorrow. They are meant to prepare you for what is to come. Ask God what is it that you need to do or work on to prepare you for marriage. Trust me no book can give you what only God can give.

The more you focus on the word, the more you will get into the plan God has for your life. Your talents are not just for you; they are for the kingdom and will benefit others. The more I focus on my relationship with Jesus, the more I am becoming the person He wants me to be. I can see the process. I don't know what's going to happen tomorrow but I know I am not the same person I was a few years ago. There is nothing more refreshing than to see what God is doing in your life.

I never knew how much my weight hindered me. Not just physically but spiritually as well. I was very insecure, lacked confidence, and was afraid to show my talents for fear that all anyone would see was the "fat" girl. I have shed 70lbs so far, and my confidence is increasing, not only in myself but in the God in me. I am realizing that my dreams are in grasp. I am also realizing that what God has for me is far beyond what I could ever ask for. What He is showing me or leading me towards, I never even knew I had the ability to accomplish. This book is one and poetry is another. I am standing in front of my church delivering original poetry. It's amazing and I have always been afraid of public speaking. In my quite time I often tell God, I don't know what you are doing, but I trust You and know You have a perfect plan. I'm certainly enjoying the ride, though it's a bit scary at times, I know that if He brought me to it, He will give me the ability to do it.

Indiana Tuggle

Stop comparing yourself to others

As singles we have to stop coveting the things of others. I want a job like so and so. I want a husband like so and so. I want to be such and such like so and so. There are two problems with this:

1. **We see the end result and don't know the journey.**
   One preacher said "You see my glory but you don't know my story." We don't know what so and so went through to get what they have. We also don't know if the road traveled was by and through God. From across the street the grass always looks greener. It's not till you get over there that you find out the grass was sprayed with that green paint or you see the many brown patches. Asking for what someone else has can also open the door to their troubles as well.

2. **God has a unique plan for all of us.**
   If we could all be like each other, there would be a bunch of clones in the world and that would be quite boring. The world would be stagnant and we certainly would not be being "fruitful and multiplying" as God commanded us to do. All of our abilities are unique and are necessary for the growth and success of the world.

Stop Asking Why Am I Single

When I started writing I wanted to be a great writer and poet like Maya Angelou. Don't get me wrong I love me some Maya Angelou, I think she is brilliant. But other than her works, I know nothing about her. I read her biography and the struggles in her past, and I quickly said, God I don't want that much pain to be a great writer and poet. But what I saw was the blessings of God despite the hurts of the past. From her story I know that God is able to turn any situation around for his glory, and that is something that I want. I know that what the devil meant to hurt and destroy me, God will use it for my good. I want the future God has specifically for me.

Comparing yourself to others or wanting what someone else has blinds you from what God is doing in your life. There is nothing wrong with wanting a role model or admiring the life of someone but to seek after that exact life is sinful behavior and will only lead to frustration and disappointment. My poems don't sound like Maya Angelou's, but does that make me less of a poet? Honestly I haven't read enough of her work to compare myself to her anyway. I only know of what I see now, the Maya Angelou who spoke at the presidential inauguration and the Maya Angelou who has been on the big screen. Another danger in comparing ourselves to others is that we don't know enough to make an informed decision. God only made one Maya Angelou and she is doing the best she can with what was given her. My job is to be the best me I can be. If you compare yourself to someone else, your personal best will never be good enough.

Don't seek advice from the ungodly

Not everyone who calls themselves Christians are actually true Christians. The bible says you will know them by their fruits. We all have friends and associates who are not living according to the word of God; like living in sin, fornicating, adultery, etc. I am not saying to be hypocritical and cut them off, as we all have things we need to work on. But what I am saying is stop complaining to these people about how lonely you are and how you really want a mate.

Whether you know it or not or whether you want to admit it or not, these people are judging you and your life style. You can not appear to be an unhappy Christian. It does not look good for your witness. If you are miserable following God, why would they want to be like you and follow God? To them you have this "holier than thou" lifestyle and attitude, yet still unhappy. Ask God for a Godly person to confide in. We all need someone we can be completely transparent with, but someone who is on the fence with their faith, should not be your confidant.

Not only can this hurt your witness but it can also hurt your walk. The bible warns us not to get weary in well doing.

If we constantly seek counsel with people whose walk is not like ours we can be easily influenced to stray. They may not come out directly and say, you might as well do this and that, you will be happy. But it will be very subtle. First you will start living vicariously through them, wanting to know every detail of their activities and/or relationship. Then you will start hanging out with them in places God has already said you do not belong. Then before you know it you have backslidden and they tell you, its ok, God understands.

God's protection does not override our free will. God never promised us being a Christian would be a bed of roses. Even if it were, you can't get to the roses without touching the thorns. We have to remember God rains on the just and the unjust. There are certain blessings that all will benefit from, but there are specific blessings available to His children, those who are obedient and follow His commandments. Anything God has for you, you must be willing to sacrifice greatly to get it. Your sacrifice may include friends and family. Everyone will not understand your journey, so you have to be willing to walk away from those who do not or try to hinder you from it. Your journey is for you and only you, you cannot drag others along.

Indiana Tuggle

Don't abort the process

And do not be conformed to this world, but be transformed by the renewing of your mind, that you may prove what is that good and acceptable and perfect will of God. - Romans 12:2

The world tells us that living a Christian life is hard and not fun, but the bible teaches us that the way of the transgressor is hard. Truth is the Christian life seems hard because we are under attack. The enemy does not like our decision to follow God and tries to embarrass Him and get us to abort the process. If you are living your life as if there is no God or refuse to believe God exists, then the enemy has no beef with you and will make it seem like your world is perfect. But the minute you profess Christ, he wages war.

God never promised us that once we got saved, life would be a walk in the park. In fact He promised us persecution for His namesake. An enemy attack is one thing, but we know that is coming and we know how to fight by staying in the word. But what about the process of becoming Christ-like, of becoming whom God created you to be? This is the process we must also not abort. The bible tells us that the word is sharper than any two edged sword. It is meant to strengthen, encourage, and also to cleanse and deliver. God uses the word to cleanse out our impurities and anything that is not like Him.

Sinful behavior is one thing. Most of us are familiar with the dos and don'ts of the Ten Commandments. But what about those character flaws that are deeply embedded, rooted in the hurts and disappointments of the past. Those flaws we picked up through life experiences in an attempt to protect ourselves from pain. Those flaws that birth continual habits we have hidden from the natural eye but don't recognize have corroded our souls. These are the things that God has to pull out of us in order for us to go to the next level in him.

The more we study the word, the more we learn about God, His character and His ways, and the more we want to please Him. The more we strive to please Him, the more we are able to see through the spiritual eye. It is through the spiritual eye that we are able to see our own imperfections. This is not a pretty sight and is certainly not a pleasant experience. It was through the word that God showed me the bitterness and anger I carried. The hurts of the past caused me to put up a barrier. The molestation left me angry at all those in my world. I was angry at my mom because she didn't protect me. Therefore I didn't trust adults and developed a "me against the world" attitude. I also developed a spirit of shame toward men and felt unworthy of love and incapable of being loved. This lack of trust and lack of self-love hindered my relationship with God. I saw God as another man in my life, non-trust worthy. I had a barrier so thick, over the years my attitude was that only

I could take care of me. So I certainly didn't trust God to take care of me.

But I love how God pursued me and was patient with me. He showed me how He would never lie to me, never hurt me, or never leave me. How He is true to His word and what He has said will surely come to pass. Again the process is not easy, because old habits die hard. Letting go and relinquishing control is like pulling teeth, there will definitely be weeping and bloodshed. But you will be better and God will be able to do a mighty work in you. The beauty of the process is the joy along the way. Like I said before, the process is never ending, it is continual unto death. But each level takes you to a higher level, from glory to glory.

The bible tells us that God chastises those whom He loves. This chastisement not only prepares us for the next level in Christ, but it also keeps us humble. Though you may have overcome and eliminated many sins in your life, truly recognizing your own imperfections helps you remain non-judgmental and sympathetic to the plight of others. The more sympathetic you are to others, the better equipped you are to helping them on their journey. Helping someone else is the great commission of being a Christian.

Serve God with expectation

Behold I set before you today a blessing and a curse: the blessing, if you obey the commandments of the Lord your God which I command you today, and the curse, if you do not obey the commandments of the Lord your God, but turn aside from the way which I command you today, to go after other gods which you have not known. - Deuteronomy 11:26-28

God rewards obedience. I know there are some religions or people who say we shouldn't "give on Sunday and expect a blessing on Monday." I believe that the issue is not in the expectation but in the timeframe. I have already said before and it is worth mentioning again, God's timing is not our timing. No amount of obedience will make God act out of season, however our expectation shows our faith and trust in Him.

God knows it is difficult to stand for righteousness in a sinful world, and your sacrifice will not go unrewarded. Expecting to be rewarded for your obedience is the joy of being a Christian. Our expectation provides us the energy to keep on fighting. It's like a parent telling a child they will be given $5 for every "A" they receive on their report card, and they can spend the money in any way they want. That child is sure to work hard in every subject and will even imagine how the money will be spent on a new toy, game or outfit. When report card day comes, they rush home waving it in the air like a flag, screaming "I made four A's." Sure the parent knows the money was an incentive that the child strived to achieve, but the effort and hard work was certainly worth the reward and the parent was happy to provide it. That's how God is. We may be after the reward, but God wants our hard work and a willing heart. In the end the victory in the achievement will outweigh the reward.

Receiving one reward, causes one to work harder for a bigger better reward. One thing I know for sure, we can't out do God, He will never run out of rewards. The bible states He is able to do exceedingly and abundantly above what we can ask or think. That's like knowing there is a surprise coming that is better than anything you can imagine. Even prisoners expect to be rewarded for good behavior, such as time off their sentence or additional privileges. So why can't Christians, and we choose to serve God?

Expecting a reward does not mean to take God for granted. All of God's blessings should be accepted with gratitude and humility. While we may know and expect the reward is coming, however we do not choose the reward. But we can rest assured we will be happy whatever the prize. God is the best example of a proud parent, He delights in blessing his children. Obedience shows our love and trust in Him, while expectation shows our hope in His promises.

...who, contrary to hope, in hope believed, so that he became the father of many nations, according to what was spoken. - Romans 4:18

Abraham was a great example of expectation and reward, of faith and hope, and of promise and trust. He was old, past his prime, God promised him a son. Because of his faith, hope and trust in that promise not only did he get a son, but he became a father of MANY nations. It is because of his faith, that we are partakers of that promise as well.

Remember what God has spoken over your life. Remember the promises he made concerning you. Believe that he is able to perform it. Hope is based on what you believe to be true. Remember God is truth. Most times we are unable to expect God or hold him to his word because of our lack of confidence in our own abilities. We must learn to take ourselves out of the equation. Success or lack thereof has nothing to do with degrees, skill, or experience; but on everything about God and the purpose instilled in you at the time of creation. Believe in the promise. Believe in He that worketh in you; it is the work of His hands, not yours, that shall accomplish the promise.

Now hope does not disappoint, because the love of God has been poured out in our hearts by the Holy Spirit who was given to us. - Romans 5:5

Indiana Tuggle

If hope does not disappoint, then disappointment comes when hope is misguided or misdirected. You are disappointed because you placed hope in the wrong one. You put hope in men, they disappointed. You put hope in yourself, you were disappointed. Why? A sinful nature cannot instill hope because of pleasure seeking. Redirect, place your hope in Christ, the Creator, rather than the created. Seek to please Him. When God is part of the thought process, for every decision, every step, you can't go wrong, if you wait on the answer. Hope is belief in what you can't see. There is no hope without God, because He is the only one who can see what you can't. He is the only one who can lead you to it. Without Him life is disappointing and frustrating.

Frustration is a result of trying to do on your own, what only God can do. Relax and let God be God. Trust Him even when you don't understand. Trust Him even when the path is unclear. Your job is to study His word. Allow him complete control and he will not disappoint. How can you continue to try to take the wheel when you don't know where you are going? A car can't have two drivers, two people cannot have control. One has to sit on the passenger side, rest, and enjoy the journey.

Chapter 5
God's Work Not Busy Work

Listen to counsel and receive instruction, that you may be wise in your latter days. There are many plans in a man's heart, Nevertheless the LORD's counsel—that will stand.
Proverbs 19:20-21

Just ask anyone and they will tell you, in order to keep your mind off finding a mate, you must keep busy. This statement in essence is true. However it is what you choose to do to occupy your time that is questionable. I have learned that whatever consumes your thoughts also controls your actions. So if we are constantly thinking about a spouse or significant other, all our actions will be in that regard.

If I were invited to a party, I would think about what I was going to wear, so as to attract any single men that would be there. Or if a friend asked me to go to an event, I would say will any guys be there because I was tired of going places filled with women. I even found myself subscribing to multiple dating sites hoping to find "the one". I would try them out one by one a month at a time, and still no match. Then in anguish and frustration, I finally asked God, "Really, I can't even meet someone online?" At that moment the Holy Ghost smacked me in the face. "This is not how I want you to live," He said, "This is not life more abundantly."

Indiana Tuggle

Live life on purpose with purpose

For those who live according to the flesh set their minds on the things of the flesh, but those who live according to the Spirit, the things of the Spirit. For to be carnally minded is death, but to be spiritually minded is life and peace. - Romans 8: 5-6

I was acting like a spoiled brat. All the searching and trying in the world was not going to make God give me my husband out of season. The flesh wants what it wants, merely out of self-gratification, but God blesses us to fulfill His purpose for us, to glorify His name, and to build the kingdom. To live life on purpose with purpose means to actively pursue what God wants us to do. Simply put it means to be obedient. But in order to do so we must first know our purpose. If you don't know your purpose, the only person who can answer that is the one who created you. Trust me when I say, God is not slow in revealing the purpose he created you for. However the key is abiding in Him, spending time in the word, praying, meditating and fasting.

Often times others recognize our purpose long before we do. This is because like spirits attract. People who need what you have will be drawn to you. Now we have to be careful in this aspect, because the devil knows who you are as well, and he will send people to abuse or use you. Just a side note: The problems and tribulations of your past have nothing to do with you. You see the enemy knows who you are, and his job is to stop, hinder, or delay your progress. But little does he know that God is using him to build character in us to do what He wants us to do.

As a child I was always naturally smart. I could grasp things quickly, especially math, and then turn around and explain them to others in simplified terms. Am I a teacher? Perhaps. Then later I discovered people would come to me for anything, advice or random information. I would get upset sometimes when people asked me questions. Then I would find myself intrigued and compelled to find the answer. Then life happened I experienced some things: molestation, early sex life, growing up in poverty, watching parents abused, and I discovered I was stronger than I could even imagine. One day God spoke to me and said "He brought me through these things to help others." But how? "Teach them how to survive and live," He replied. What one goes through is not as important as coming out and moving forward. So many people are living in pain and in return are stuck in mediocrity. Who to help and how to help is still a journey, but each day God reveals a different part of the plan. But we have to remember; that once we complete one step God will reveal the next.

Writing this book was one of my steps, but because I wanted to know what the next step was, I procrastinated. Then the Holy Ghost revealed I was holding up my own blessings! When we do not do what God wants us to do, we are being disobedient. Most Christians define disobedience in one aspect: breaking the Ten Commandments. But disobedience is refusing to do anything that God has told you to do. Procrastination is disobedience as well. Procrastination just says to God "I want to do what I want to do right now and I'll do what you want me to do later." Anything that takes you away from or out of God's plan is a distraction to keep you from the true blessings of God.

As singles should we keep busy? Absolutely, but only in doing what God has for us to do. Remember singles, we have a special place in God's heart. Married people are concerned with pleasing their spouses, but singles are concerned with pleasing the Lord. God's hand is not still concerning you, He knows what you desire, but He requires your obedience. If you are unsure of your purpose, start praying, try going to your pastor and getting busy in the church. Sometimes we have to try a few things before we find our groove. Generally our purpose is that thing we do in our free time, when no one is watching, it is effortless and we rarely realize we are doing anything. It is the thing that you would do whether you got paid for it or not.

In order to begin working toward our purpose, we must first get rid of the barriers that prevent us from completely surrendering to God. These barriers cause frustration. As I stated earlier, frustration is a result of trying to do in our own strength what only God can do. If we are still relying on our own strength we cannot be used by God. To serve God is to die to self, He requires sacrifice. Lip service will no longer do. Lip service leaves you stagnant, lazy, and procrastinating. But God is requiring action; your soul is crying for movement. This is why we are unhappy, standing still yet afraid to move. The inability to move is because we have not surrendered all. God requires control in every area of our lives, not just those areas that we feel we can't handle. To love God is to trust Him; to trust Him is to know Him. You can't know Him without spending time with Him.

What's true in the natural is generally true in the spirit. To get to know someone in the natural you spend time with them, hang out, talk on the phone, etc. However when it comes to getting to know God, we want it to happen overnight. We cannot physically go to heaven and spend time with God. But he requires us to commune with him. John 1:1 says "in the beginning was the word, the word was with God, and the word was God." In other words everything we need to know and want to know about God is in the word. Praying alone is not going to cut it. Without the word, prayers are empty and full of materialistic requests. Without the word, we prohibit God from speaking to us, thus preventing His power from working in our lives.

Indiana Tuggle

Understand what prevents you from drawing closer to God

Relationship is the key to being able to surrender. Like I said earlier, before we can surrender, we must first address the barriers preventing us from drawing closer to Him:

1. **Loneliness**

   There is no sin in feeling lonely. God created us for relationship and to want to commune with others. However loneliness causes us to seek after love in all the wrong places. Loneliness causes us to search for in others, what only God can give.

   God is love. There is no greater love than the love of God. No one will ever love you more than, or at the same magnitude as the love of God. God loves us. Period. There is nothing we could do or not do for Him to stop loving us. However we must know that He loves us, hear that He loves us, see that He loves us, and abide in His love. To abide in God's love means to stop trying to earn His love. It is impossible, and to try to do so, leaves us empty and more frustrated.

   God chose us. Not the other way around. He chose us before placing us in our mother's womb. That choice was made with full awareness of the mistakes we would make before we accepted Him as our Savior. Our past was just a instrument He used to draw us into the acknowledgement that we needed Him. It is not the end of our journey. God is bigger than anything we have seen and greater than what we can imagine. The love you seek is within, because Jesus lives in you. God knew you needed Him before you knew of Him. While you were searching for love, love was searching for you. He is ready to give that love to you, but you must allow Him to increase. In order for God to increase you must decrease, you must surrender to His control.

How do we overcome loneliness? The plan to overcome loneliness may be different for many. However here are a few basic steps. First, be honest with God. God cannot help you without complete honesty. Honesty says two things: (1) I recognize the issue and (2) I need God's help. Until you admit those two things, God cannot help. Remember God gives us free will, He is a gentleman He does not force himself on us, yet He is eager to assist when we call. Second acknowledge the things that loneliness causes you to do and try them against the word. Loneliness is the root of many issues. We must recognize the power and control it has on our lives. Once it is exposed we can counterattack. I am still learning how loneliness affects my life. Loneliness was the root of my obesity. I ate because I was lonely. Food was my friend. I ate when I was sad, happy and bored. Once you recognize the problems allow God to snatch them out at the root. Lastly, acknowledge that to be lonely is not the same as being alone. Lonely is a feeling. You may feel lonely sometimes but you are never alone. God promised to never leave nor forsake you. There are times in your life when God wants you to be alone. Let's face it there are things in life we must go through alone, but we must remember God is always there.

2. **Fear**

Fear is the most damaging four-letter word to the life of a Christian. It is debilitating. It weighs us down because it brings a lot of friends with it. With fear comes regret, shame, low self-esteem, pity, failure, anger, resentment, unforgiveness, etc. Movement or action is a big part of the Christian life. We must hear the word of the Lord and act upon it. But anything the enemy can use to stop us from moving, he will do so. Fear is one of those stop signs. Fear uses mistakes and experiences of the past to hold you from your future.

I was talking to a friend recently about my past molestation issues. She asked me was I still angry with my mother. I can now honestly say I am not. I used to blame my mom because she did not protect me or get me any help. I realized though that the first two times it happened I didn't tell anyone. So how can someone get you help for something they knew nothing about? Then I realized my mother also had an abusive past, and she probably did what she knew to do or thought was appropriate. One day we had a conversation and I asked her why we never discussed the molestation (the one she knew about) and she said I never brought it up so she didn't either. Then I came to the realization that she thought she was giving me my space to heal and that talking about it would be like snatching the Band-Aid off the womb. Or she just simply didn't know what to do, maybe that's how her mom handled it when it happened to her.

Then my friend asked me, was I angry towards my Dad. Not really, my Dad is a whole different story. You see I have two Dads. Dad #1, who is also my brother's father, is the one who raised me. He was an alcoholic and cocaine addict. I saw this man beat my mother, sell drugs and he even got my mother addicted to cocaine. Dad #2, was kind of like a thought in the back of my mind. Going to school my mom would put his name on the paperwork, but I had never met him. Then when I was about 13, I was able to put a face to the name. It was literally a "hi how are you" and that was it. He made some promises about coming back for my birthday but I never saw him again.

Then when I was 30, I needed a passport but my birth certificate was illegible and I needed another copy. So I went to the health department to get one and they couldn't find my name. Finally the woman asked for my mother's name and my date of birth. She found me and then told me my name had been changed to my father's last name, which was Dad #2. By now I'm all dramatic saying "how can someone just change my name?" I don't know this man and he has never done anything for me, I don't want his name. To make a long story short, I kept my mother's name. But I inquired about him to my mother and she said she had lost touch with him, but knew the neighborhood where his brother lived. We went to the apartment and Dad #2 answered the door. I had mixed emotions. I was angry and felt abandoned. Then I was relived, that the horrible Dad #1 was not really my father, and perhaps God was giving me a second chance at a real father daughter relationship. The he started again with the empty promises. We didn't spend any time together; nor did he allow me to meet my other brothers and sisters. I was truly disappointed, but I never said anything, I just said ok whenever we did speak. So perhaps I do have abandonment issues with my dad, but not regarding the molestation.

My problem with the molestation is I don't know who to blame. In my head it has to be someone's fault. I came to a conclusion that the young girls from the first two molestations were just children and probably doing what they had been taught or perceived to be right, so it wasn't their fault. It wasn't my mother's fault, because she didn't know. And it wasn't my fault because I too was a child. Before I blamed myself because

I was looking for love and friendship and felt I allowed myself to be used. God told me it wasn't my fault. So whose fault is it? I don't know how to process "it's no one's fault." Who am I forgiving if it's no one's fault? Am I forgiving myself for holding on to the baggage all these years?

This is what fear does. It makes you hold on to the past, afraid of what the future might hold pain free. I know pain and lack. I have lived with them my whole life. But happiness and success, I know nothing about. Letting go of the pain and suffering meant opening a door to the unknown. I feared the unknown. I don't know what happiness feels like and therefore was afraid of giving up the control I thought I had. But we do not control fear, it controls us.

Happiness is not a feeling. Happy is a feeling. Happy is dependent upon an event, thing, or person. The "y" in happy, stands for "you", you (someone else) must make me happy. On the other hand happiness is a state of being happy. The suffix "ness" added to happy turned the word from an adjective to a noun. But the revelation that God gave me about happiness is that in order to go from happy to happiness, we must change the "y" to an "I". In other words, we must go from relying on others to make us happy to relying on self. We transition from "you make me happy" to "I make me happy". Then God told me about the two p's of happiness that are required to remain in the constant state of happy. They are purpose and power. We must know the purpose God created us for and actively pursue it using the power of Jesus Christ within us. This is our life's journey and in doing so, we will remain in happiness.

There is no happiness living in fear. A prophetess came to our church one Sunday. She stated that "do not fear" is found in the bible 365 times. Wow, so every day, God gave us a "do not fear". For God to repeat a phrase that many times, it must really be important. Daily we must not fear and choose to pursue happiness. Our fore fathers had it right. Our constitution says "all have the right to life, liberty, and the pursuit of happiness." To pursue something means to actively seek to obtain it. This requires action and again fear cannot coexist with action. As fear keeps you stuck in one place, afraid to move forward because you are too busy looking back.

For God has not given us a spirit of fear, but of power and of love and of a sound mind. - 1 Timothy 1:7

How do we eliminate fear? Since fear did not come from God, we must send it back to its owner. Return to sender! So who is the blame for the molestations of my past? The enemy, that's who. It had nothing to do with me, but about the kingdom. The enemy was trying to prevent me from becoming the woman God created me to be. But little did he know that the same painful experiences he threw in my way to hold me back are the same experiences God will use to pull someone else into the light. The best way to fight the enemy is to expose the lie. The lie was me taking the blame and living a life of fear and shame.

The truth is there are things in life that happen to us not because we have done wrong but because God wants to show us His power and His ability to work a miracle in our lives. God is the light in the darkness of our past. (John 1:5) Once we understand that, He is able to shine and use us to bless others.

3. **Identity**

Identity is a two-fold issue. First in order to surrender we must know who God is. His character, His love, His faithfulness, His power, and His sovereignty all help us understand Him and trust Him to rule over our lives.

"God is not a man, that He should lie, nor a son of man, that He should repent. Has He said, and will He not do? Or has He spoken, and will He not make it good? - Numbers 23:19

God is not like man. He does not lie to us, hurt us, manipulate us, disappoint us, or sell us empty promises, etc. Our experiences with man, give a false misrepresentation of who God is. This is why fathers are so important to God. Fathers are our first encounters of authority figures on the earth. If this authority is abused or misused, those to follow will be filtered through those experiences. Fathers are also to be teachers of the gospel. Fathers are to teach their children of the goodness of the Lord, so that the children will learn to rely and trust Him. Failure to do so results in a loveless generation.

Lack of good role models cause us to view God through those same dirty lenses. So if our earthly fathers did not correctly teach us who God is, then we must rely on the testimony of His character found in the bible. We are strengthened by the testimony of others, but there is nothing like learning who God is for yourself. How do we learn about God? It is through our afflictions that we know Him. In the bible God says for us to try him and he will show himself approved. Test me and see says the Lord.

I am a tither, and my church also believes in first fruit. Annually we give unto the Lord our first weeks' pay. So whatever our take home check was for the first week in January, we give as a sacrificial offering unto the Lord, in April. This offering is a statement of trust in the Lord to provide for us throughout the year. During first fruit service we hear testimonies from others of how God went above and beyond to provide for them and their families. Well last year I shared my first fruit testimony. In 2010 I thought I was going to lose my house. To be honest, I could have paid my house note, but it was a struggle. I couldn't get overtime at work and the bills were increasing. The price of gas was rising and the utility bills seemed to double. I asked the mortgage company for help but they refused since I was not behind. So I took matters in my own hands and decided not to pay, and they would help me. One month turned to three months and three months to six months, and now I was facing foreclosure.

I tried to go through a home save program, but they had me submitting all kinds of paperwork only to say I had enough income to pay the mortgage. Which was true at first, but six months behind, I could not afford to catch up. I cried and I prayed and I cried and I prayed. Then a peace came over me like a mighty wind and all I heard the Lord say was trust me. By now I am thinking, God I have no choice, because there is nothing I can do. So I said whatever you decide God, I will be content, if I stay in my home or if I have to leave, I will still praise you. I would love to say that I remained in this peace. But I have to admit, that it got tough. Amazingly though, I can only remember getting a debt collection call from the mortgage company twice through the whole ordeal. Well six months turned to ten months. I finally received my modification in the mail. My interest rate dropped from 7.125% to 5.5% and my payments also dropped by $200. My new payments were at a 40-year fixed rate, but I didn't lose my house! It's been a year since and my credit has been restored. Through it all I can say, God is faithful even when we are not. I could have lost my house and I was prepared to take the blame and suffer the consequences. But God said No. God showed me He was my provider.

I have lived alone most of my adult life. About two years ago I had a break in. Whenever I think of that day, I thank God. I was late for work. So I decided to call-in and just take the day off, get caught up on some housework and school work. I had just gotten out the shower, called my manager, and was about to get back in the bed. Before my head hit the pillow I got a phone call saying my grandmother was in the hospital. She had suffered a stroke. I jumped up, put on clothes and went to the hospital. On the way I called two church members and asked them to pray. Then I began to pray, and heard the Lord say just lay your hands on her, she will be ok. I stayed at the hospital about two hours until they got her in stable condition. I came back home to find, my home had been broken into. The robbers stole a flat-screen TV, a laptop and a cell phone. All this was in broad day light. I just think about, if God had not allowed me to leave, I would have been home during the intrusion and could have been harmed, raped or even murdered. In that instance God showed me He was my protector.

I said all that to say, that God allows things to happen in our lives not to punish us but to show us who He is and His love for us. The experiences are sometimes necessary to counteract the false messages instilled in us by the pains of our past experiences and relationships.

The second part of identity, that prevents us from surrendering to God, is failure to know who we are. Sometimes the painful experiences of the past, leaves us with low self-worth. We feel our lives are worthless and unworthy of love, success and happiness. Until we see and acknowledge the beauty of creation in us, we are unable to be fully used by God. Before we can help others we must first obtain help ourselves.

A big part of this identity crisis is the inability to accept forgiveness. Once we ask for forgiveness with sincerity of heart, God forgives us and throws it into a sea of forgetfulness. This is another reason why knowing God's character and who He is is important. Again He is not like man. He will not say He forgives us and then bring it back up every chance he gets. We cannot serve God according to worldly understanding. Serving God is not limited to obeying the Ten Commandments. God's righteousness requires personal relationship, understanding of His character and unconditional love. The righteousness of God is love, trust and forgiveness. Worldly knowledge says that when you mess up you are a bad Christian or fall out of God's grace. But the righteousness of God says repent, and it is because of His grace that you are forgiven and can continue on the journey He has set before you. Guilt and shame causes you to stop, give up, and have a pity party.

God's purpose for your life does not change when you mess up. Your purpose was written in stone before birth with the knowledge of your mistakes along the way. The inability to accept forgiveness keeps you stagnant. Constantly asking for forgiveness crucifies God over and over again. Believe in your heart the first time and no others are necessary. Thank Him and move on.

It is one thing to know who you are and another to walk in who you are. You are the righteousness of Christ. His blood shed on the cross declared you righteous. Be conscious of this fact. When you are conscious of everything that appears to be wrong in your life, you hide from God. You are the chosen of Christ. He chose you from the beginning. Accept His choice, acknowledge the call, and allow Him to show you what He wants you to do.

The inability to move forward is because of the lack of knowledge in who you are. Movement is tied to identity. Allow God to show you who you are, who you are in Him, and who He is in you. Then you will know and understand where you are going. You must stop aborting the process. Before God will allow you to move, He must first mold you into the person He knows and created you to be. He is the potter, we are the clay. Until we take form we are of no use to the world.

4. Disobedience

Therefore you must be subject, not only because of wrath but also for conscious' sake. - Romans 13:5

There is no rest in disobedience. God's peace cannot abide in a disobedient heart. Therefore we must quicken when we hear the voice of the Lord. Most Christians think of obedience in reference to what not to do. But the Ten Commandments are the basics. God's commandments consist of anything He has told us to do. There are many blessings attached to the obedience of God, but there are repercussions to disobedience as well. Faith in God should move us into action.

God speaks in the now, if He tells us to do something He means now. What about preparation? As in the natural, anything done in the Spirit will require preparation. Christians have gotten it backwards though, preparation does not mean wait or do nothing. When God reveals his purpose for us, he will also give us the steps to take to get there. Joseph had the dream he would be king or ruler over many years before it came to pass. Joseph didn't stop believing and didn't lose hope when he was thrown in the dungeon or into prison. It is not what happens to us, but how we respond to it that determines our destiny. Trials and tribulations are sometimes the preparation for the blessings of the Lord. It is those very trials that God uses to produce character, and bless others. So when we stop and give up during the hard times, we are keeping God from not only delivering us but delivering others as well.

We are God in the Earth. He lives inside of us. If we don't move, He can't move. The word promises us that God's word will not return to Him void. God is not going to beg us to do what he called us to do. If we refuse he will raise up a whole new generation to accomplish the task. There is no worse feeling than to see someone else do what God called you to do. You are capable of accomplishing the task. God does not tell you to do something and then not show you how to complete it. Know your purpose and know that it is the power of God in you that will enable you to perform it.

Who are you to judge another's servant? To his own master he stands or falls. Indeed he will be made to stand, for God is able to make him stand.- Romans 14:4

We are sometimes our own worst critics. We tell ourselves what we can't do before we even try. Failure is not an option in Christ. Who are you to judge what God created? He created you and therefore know what you are capable of. It is only in your own eyes that you fail. For in God's eyes you are strong and victorious. It is because of God, through his strength, that you are able to finish any task. But you must be willing to let him show you how to do it. Don't give up, constantly stopping, complaining, etc. is preventing forward progress. God does not make you start over, your own insecurities make you start over. God is waiting to forgive you and continue in the journey.

We have all heard the cliché, "If at first you don't succeed, try, try again." This may be true in the simplest terms in that one must not be afraid of failure. But God can do anything but fail. If we fail it is because we are trying to achieve the goal in our own strength. If we truly allow God to order our footsteps, we cannot fail.

Chapter 6
Happiness Comes From God

You have put gladness in my heart, more than in the season that their grain and wine increased.
Psalm 4:7

The word says God put gladness in our hearts, yet we still are not happy. So what happened to the joy God gave us at creation? It is still there however we have allowed it to be covered up with the hurts and concerns of our daily struggles. As Christians we already know we are not of this world. So then why do we seek happiness as those of the world do? The world says happiness is found in material possessions, wealth, status, power, etc. But God says happiness is in Him. Therefore our lack of happiness derives from seeking things rather than God. We also refuse to seek God because of low self-worth.

Recognize who you are

The first step in recognizing who you are is admitting that you have been deceived. Hurtful experiences of the past, misinterpreted love and affection from others, ill-intentions, or just lack of knowledge have all contributed to the deceit. It is important to realize that all the wounding words, situations and people, who provided a sense of false identity, were in fact liars. The next step is to uncover the truth. The truth is in the word:

Blessed be the God and Father of our Lord Jesus Christ, who has blessed us with every spiritual blessing in the heavenly places in Christ, just as He chose us in Him before the foundation of the world, that we should be holy and without blame before Him in love, having predestined us to adoption as sons by Jesus Christ to Himself, according to the good pleasure of His will, to the praise of the glory of His grace, by which He made us accepted in the Beloved. In Him we have redemption through His blood, the forgiveness of sins, according to the riches of His grace which He made to abound toward us in all wisdom and prudence, having made known to us the mystery of His will, according to His good pleasure which He purposed in Himself, that in the dispensation of the fullness of the times He might gather together in one all things in Christ, both which are in heaven and which are on earth—in Him. In Him also we have obtained an inheritance, being predestined according to the purpose of Him who works all things according to the counsel of His will, that we who first trusted in Christ should be to the praise of His glory. In Him you also trusted, after you heard the word of truth, the gospel of your salvation; in whom also, having believed, you were sealed with the Holy Spirit of promise, who is the guarantee of our inheritance until the redemption of the purchased possession, to the praise of His glory. - Ephesians 1: 3-14

You are holy and without blame. (vs. 4) God sees and is only concerned with your obedience to His will. He finds no fault in you. You are His adopted child. (vs. 5) He chose you. You are accepted. (vs. 6) He wants you just as you are. You are redeemed and forgiven. (vs. 7) He already paid the price for your mistakes on the cross and threw your sins into a sea of forgetfulness. You have an inheritance and are predestined for greatness. (vs. 11) His death gave you immediate access to your blessings. He created you with a purpose. You are sealed with a promise. (vs. 13) God does not break promises, if He said it, it shall come to pass. You are a purchased possession. (vs. 14) You belong to God.

You are of great value. God created you, He wanted you, and He died for you. Recognize who you are in Him. Not who you think you are according to words spoken by others in the past or who you think you should be according to unrealistic or unconsented goals or dreams. Money, material possessions, status or opinions from others do not define who you are. God defined who you were at creation. You were made in His image, with a plan.

When God looks at you, He sees Himself. You are who He says you are. Believe His words, repeat His words, and meditate on His words. Joy comes in the celebration of God's greatest creation…YOU. Open your spiritual eyes and look in the mirror of your soul, there you will see God. You will see the greatness of His power and the beauty of you as His creation.

We are sometimes our own worst critics and thus the most damaging to our own self-worth. How often do we find ourselves repeating the very same words that hurt us when spoken by others? "I'm lazy, I can't do nothing right, I'm weak, I can't do this, I can't do that, I'm not as pretty or as handsome as him or her, or I'm ugly." These words go directly against the word of God. The bible tells us our words are spirit and life. When we repeat such ugliness we give life to it and thus make it become true because we act them out by living in mediocrity.

You have to be great in your own eyes, before you can be great in someone else's. It's all in the eye of the beholder: greatness, beauty, love, significance, and happiness. If you don't see it in yourself, no one else will. Until you recognize who you are, unfortunately you are not ready to be used by God. You cannot love God or others, until you love yourself. Love covers a multitude of sins. Love sees no fault, knows no weakness, and encompasses hope for tomorrow. Tomorrow has endless possibilities with God in control.

A co-worker asked me to speak at her church for the youth black history program. The first thing that came out of my mouth, instantly with no thought, was "I am not successful." She said "yes you are, you are such an inspiration" and asked me to think about it. I prayed about it and the first thing the Holy Ghost whispered in my spirit was "how dare you sit down on what the Lord has done, look how far you have come." I didn't really look at my life as "how far I'd come" but rather where I've been and how far I have to go. I have been used, abused, molested, mistreated, etc. I don't have the career, husband, or family I want. I saw my life as one extreme to the next: the horrible experiences of the past and the failures of the future. How could the future be a failure, when it hadn't come yet? I forgot about the present. I forgot about the health, job, home, two degrees, and working on a third that the Lord has blessed me with in the present. We place so much pressure on ourselves to obtain goals that we forget to celebrate the journey. Who did I consult with when I told myself at 18 that I would be married and have 2.5 children and a career by 30? Certainly not God. Why do we deny ourselves happiness for failure to reach goals we have no control over?

I decided to speak at my friend's church. I took the advice of another friend and did not prepare a speech but rather spoke from the heart. I told them the testimony of the past, what I had been through and the abuse I saw in my family. I also told them about how my mother may not have been a Christian but she knew to send me to church. Then I didn't know what I was doing by writing in my journal, "dear God," but today I know I was establishing a relationship with Him. At 17 I was surrounded by drugs, violence, and watched little girls get pregnant at 15, go on welfare and move into their own apartment in the same projects at age 18. I knew I wanted better but I didn't know what better was. God had to show me and guide me. Yes I messed up and took a few wrong turns along the way, but I have to trust God and know that where I am is exactly where He wants me to be. As long as I have breath in my body, I will never stop dreaming. Because of my relationship with Jesus, I know that I can't out dream God, if He put it in me, I know He can show me how to make it come to pass. It is dreaming that keeps me motivated and striving for better, and it is my faith and trust in God that allows me to enjoy the journey.

Realizing who you are means understanding your position and purpose in God. His death on the cross declared us righteous, believing in this fact and having faith in Him, gave Him access and control in our lives. He created us for a purpose, we have to allow Him to reveal that purpose and take us to that place by any means necessary. We are predestined for greatness, but we have to relinquish control back to the creator.

Realizing who you are also means accepting that you are where you should be in life. God does not make mistakes. The experiences of the past, good or bad were preordained by God to get you to today. At the end of that service, many of the members came up to me, hugging me and some in tears, expressing how my testimony blessed them and gave them the encouragement they needed to keep going and continue the fight.

It wasn't really about you. The devil tried to keep you down, but God wants to use that very thing to bring someone else out. But you have to stop living in the pain and regret. Let go of the "why me" mentality. Stop questioning God. Instead ask "why not me?" Even if it was too horrible for you to believe God ordained it, you must realize that He allowed it. It is bigger than you, it's about the kingdom. You are able to help others let go of the pain. In order to help someone else, you have to go through it so you can 1. Empathize with them and 2. Show them the correct way out.

Believe His word

For we are His workmanship, created in Christ Jesus for good works, which God prepared beforehand that we should walk in them.- Ephesians 2:10

Believe in God, believe in His word, and believe in His word concerning you. Regardless of what happened in the past, you are His workmanship. Regardless of the mistakes you made, you were created for good works. Regardless of fear, you must walk in the path He has for you. Believe that He is with you always. God is not concerned about the past. He is the present and is leading you to a greater future. Believe in the ability He has given you. You are more than capable. He knows what He put in you and He knows what you can handle. Believe in yourself because you are His chosen vessel, His creation, His mouthpiece, and His most precious child.

The word says we should not think more highly of ourselves than we ought to. This is pride and we know pride has no place in God. But I believe that as Christians we sometimes take that statement to the extreme. It is true we can do nothing without God. But the word also says "I can do all things through Christ Jesus which strengthens me." Which means it is the strength of God in us, not His strength influencing the world around us. Faith means we have confidence in the God in us. We are capable of anything and can accomplish anything in God's strength. We should live an attitude of victory knowing that God is with us.

I never understood Christians who end every statement or prayer with "if it be your will." Now I understand "if it be your will" is a cop out. It is actually fear based. I once heard a prophetess preach on this very same thing. She said that "if it be your will" indicates you have no expectancy, so if it does not work out, you will not be disappointed. As Christians we are called by His name, His death, resurrection and our acceptance of Him as our Lord and Savior declared us righteous, therefore we are in His will. The only thing that separates us from His will is sin, but because of His grace we can ask for forgiveness and get right back into His will. So if we are already in His will, rather than praying "if it be your will," we should come before the throne with boldness making our requests known declaring what His word says. Nothing moves God to action more than repeating His word back to Him, because His word will not return to Him void. If it's in the word, He is obligated to make it happen.

But if we don't believe what the word says we are unable to repeat it with boldness. We question it and ponder over it. We also spend too much time trying to discover hidden meanings. God is not that complicated. Just do it. He will not let you fail. He is waiting on you to make a step, to take a stand, and to decide to trust Him. Just go. As you go, He will strengthen you. As you go, you will leave fear behind. As you go, you will understand the fullness of who you are and where you are going. As you go, He will make your enemies your footstool.

Trust that you are lacking nothing. Everything you need was placed in you at creation. You are not weak, for in God you are strong. You are already victorious. Look at where He has brought you from. God has always been with you; He never left you. Believe in yourself, who you were, who He created you to be, who you are now and who He is preparing you to be. You are holding yourself back, trust in God, trust His word and He will show you the way.

Just do it. Do what God has told you to do. Read and study His word. Don't question it. Fight not to give up. Your latter will be much greater. Happiness is the reward of doing what God called you to do. Believe that you are walking in your purpose right now and that He is well pleased. Happiness is not in acquiring money or material things, nor in doing something great. Great is the man who is obedient to God's word. Trust and know that you are already great in His eyes. Greater works you will do. Greater is He that is in you, than he that is in the world. Stop living life according to what could be. Happiness is realizing who you already are.

Stay the course

Therefore I ask that you do not lose heart at my tribulations for you, which is your glory. - Ephesians 3:13

As Christians we need to toughen up, myself included. God never promised us the road would be easy. Christian life is not all sugar and candy. It is the end prize that we must remember. We have to remember the ultimate promise of eternal life with Him and having life more abundantly while we are here. Yet in the midst of the trial, these promises are the furthest from our mind. But God implores us to not lose heart.

Don't despise what you went through, for it is that very thing that will exalt you among the people and qualify you for God's service. The fight is not just about you, that's why it's important not to give up. You are fighting for others as well. Others who are still condemned by their past, living in fear, afraid to live, afraid to ask for help, and afraid to go to Jesus.

Others who don't even know they need help and have become content with mediocrity, pain, sadness, and hopelessness. You are God's example. You are living proof of God's power to overcome, to be victorious, and to be happy. Others are dependent on you. Your pain will produce fruit.

The problem with some Christians is that they are not willing to share their pains and heartaches of the past. With every test, there is a testimony. But we want the world to believe that we were born Christians, never sinned, and live in Mr. Rogers neighborhood. Some leave out the details and may speak in broad terms, using words such as "we have all sinned, but God is able to help us out of everything." What we have to realize is that when someone is hurting, the hurt isolates them. One thinks they are alone in the world and that their problem is the worst thing that ever happened and no one can relate. As Christians, by keeping our testimony hidden we are not revealing the specific problems and how God brought us out. The world is longing for that personal relationship with God. They want to know the God who is concerned about all their problems and who can help them find a way out. They also need to know that the process is not overnight.

The process is the most important part of the journey. It separates the boys from the men, so to speak. How you go through depends on how soon you give it to God and how you follow directions afterward. This was a hard pill to swallow for me. The pain in my life caused me to build a wall no one could penetrate. I trusted no one, and I had a "me against the world" attitude. I felt like a Christian, but I saw God as this untouchable being looking down on us, watching us live our lives.

I never thought of God as someone I could commune with. Yes I talked to Him, but I never knew or thought He would respond back. I saw Him like the many men in my life that had hurt me. I did not know how to receive His love nor give Him love in return. I also thought that my pain made me dirty, unworthy, and undeserving of love from anyone, especially God. This unworthiness caused me to pull away when God was drawing me closer. Though I may have written to God in my diary or prayed on occasion, I rarely opened my bible except when in church.

Once I began reading the word, God started talking to me. It was amazing. My notebook became filled with revelations of the word that He gave me from those readings, words about my future, how He loved me and would erase my past and use me to help others. But when God started to uncover the hurt, I would pull away. I would stop reading and stop praying, thinking that He would just let me be. I was stubborn. I realize now that in order for God to heal the hurt He has to uncover the pain. Sometimes we become so accustomed to the pain that we don't even realize how it affects our lives. The pain affected my self-esteem, my self-worth, and paralyzed me. It even affected my weight. I have big dreams but I was afraid to try, afraid to fail, and afraid to succeed. I was stuck.

But because I felt like I was stuck, I felt like I was disappointing God. I felt He was fed up with me starting and stopping. I felt He was tired of me running. I learned running is not a sign of failure. Running is a sign that the process is working. Running lets us know that the spirit man and the flesh are warring. The spirit man wants to be healed and to be free. The flesh wants things to stay the same and continue being comfortable in the familiar. Running is human and it is normal. But it is the thinking that, I had to start all over again, every time I came back that God wanted to remove. God doesn't make us start over; it is our own thoughts that make us start over. God is ready to pick up the pieces and start where He left off.

In home remodeling or renovation, they say it has to get ugly before it gets pretty. This is true for deliverance as well. I used to jokingly say "the more I read the word, the more I discover I'm not as cute as I thought I was." It was because the hurt had hardened my heart and I recognized I was decaying on the inside. God was working on the inside, creating in me a clean heart. Running may be normal, but it is the easy way out. Staying the course produces patience and strength. We have to fight not to abort the process. Knowing that it is not just about me and that my future depends on it, helps me to stay on track. Staying the course also produces trust and tests our faith. Only God knows when the course is completed. We have to have confidence in Him that He will do what he promised us He would do. Happiness is in the expectation of a reward at the end.

Watch what you say

Let no corrupt word proceed out of your mouth, but what is good for necessary edification, that it may impart grace to the hearers. - Ephesians 4:29

When we think about watching what we say, gossiping is the first thing that comes to mind. However not only should you watch what you say concerning others, but you especially must watch what you say concerning yourself. God is living inside you. He is the "Great I Am." "I Am" is His name. Anytime you use "I Am", God rises and angels are sent on assignment to complete the task that proceeds it. Negative or positive, because you said it, it must come to pass. When the task is negative, it is like crying wolf. It is a false calling and God returns disappointed because you still don't understand who you are. You don't understand the strength inside you. You don't understand the power you carry as His namesake. The Angels are jealous of you, because you look like Him and

He has relinquished power in the earth to you. Yet you do not use it. You are God in the Earth. Things happen at the sound of your voice.

You have the power to change today and tomorrow, beginning with how you speak concerning yourself. Life and death is in the power of the tongue. Positive words provide life and produce motivation. Negative words kill happiness and corrode the soul. You were not created for mediocrity. Greatness is you, because "I Am" is great in you. No longer allow the enemy to distort your worth. The blood, your acceptance, and your belief make you worthy.

Stay in your lane

That we should no longer be children, tossed to and fro and carried about with every wind of doctrine, by trickery of men, in the cunning craftiness of deceitful plotting. - Ephesians 4:14

Let's just keep it real, at some point we need to stop asking and start doing. Enough with the "are you sure Lord?" and "Lord if that's you give me a sign." God is not the author of confusion. Your purpose is not a mystery. It is not hidden from you, in fact God has been telling you the same thing over and over. Stop questioning God. Stop questioning your ability. Stop questioning His timing. Stop asking when or how. Questioning God only wastes time. Time that you could be doing what He told you to do.

Indiana Tuggle

We are supposed to not only be hearers but also doers of the word. Faith is in the doing, not in the asking. In fact if your mouth is still moving, you are not doing anything. Questioning distracts the driver. Ouch! That cut me deep. I have a problem with going places and I don't know where I am going. If I am driving out of town, I need my directions, address of the hotel, addresses of the places I am going, all before I pull out my drive way. Even if I am following someone, I need my own directions. God forbid they take a wrong turn or I get lost in traffic. Now if I am not driving, I am a little more relaxed. I don't need directions; I just need to know the itinerary. And if we deviate from the itinerary, I usually will have an attitude. Not knowing where I am going causes anxiety for me. I must be in control.

This is a problem with God. We are to blindly follow Him. We are to relinquish control to Him. Questioning Him is a form of control. If you are still questioning, then you have no faith in Him. God cannot work where there is no faith. To stay in your lane you have to let God be God. He does not need your help.

To stay in your lane also means to stick to what God has you to do. Even as Christians we can be jealous or covet the anointing of others. Why can't I do this and that like sister or brother so and so? Why sister or brother so and so always doing that. Like I said, if you are talking you are probably not doing anything. If we tell the truth, sister or brother so and so probably doing everything because you are not doing your job and they are wearing too many hats. Which brings me to another point, if you stay in your lane you impact those around you. Others can focus on their specific calling instead of doing something they are not called to do. Driving in two lanes can cause an accident.

A lot of time we focus on others because we feel what God has called us to do is not as glamorous or as important as so and so. But we have to remember, gifts and calling are for the edification of the church. We are all one church, one body. Everybody can't be a head, an arm or a leg. Someone has to be a toe, a finger, or even a fingernail or toenail. But all are needed for proper functioning.

When one part does not function, it causes the other parts to go into overload to compensate for the missing part. Think about it. We have five senses. If we lose one, the others become stronger. People who are deaf, have the most amazing sense of touch. They can feel the vibration of the ground or floor when someone is walking towards them. But in the church body, this can cause the other members to become burned out or tired. Sister or brother so and so may not always want to be doing this and that. But because they love the Lord and do not want the ministry to suffer, they will do this and that even though God called them to do something else.

You will be held accountable for your gift. We all know the parable of the talents. Do you want the Lord to say well done thy good and faithful servant? God is not going to hold us accountable for what someone else does. But the moment he reveals your purpose, it is our duty to accomplish it in the Earth.

Some questions are important. Such as when Mary asked (concerning her getting pregnant) "how could this be when I haven't known a man?" Sometimes the calling God places on us may seem outrageous or too difficult. But I find the best question is "what's the first step?" Nothing is impossible or too difficult for God.

God is a God of order. At the completion of each step the next will be revealed. Happiness is found in the obedience of completing each task. There is no greater joy than knowing you are in His will. Questioning does not make Him move faster. I believe it angers God because it shows lack of trust and faith. Trust His voice. Trust His word. Trust the process. He will not lead you astray or allow you to fall. Remember He can do anything but fail. Failure only comes with ignoring His voice. If we belong to Him and spend time with Him, we should know His voice. The bible says "my sheep know my voice." If you are still questioning His voice, either your relationship with Him is slacking or you are trying to do things your way on your own.

Seek to please the Lord

For you were once darkness, but now you are light in the Lord. Walk as children of light...finding out what is acceptable to the Lord. - Ephesians 5: 8, 10

To put it more simply: now that you know better, do better. Nothing can destroy your happiness faster, than continually trying to do wrong when you know what's right. It's called the Holy Spirit. The job of the Holy Spirit is to keep you in line. When you stray, here comes the rod of correction. If you refuse, He will make you miserable. Once you belong to God, you no longer get away with anything.

I have to be honest. Sometimes I wish I could lie. It would make it easier, as I wouldn't have to answer all those questions. Well I thought it was easier to lie. Until I realized you have to remember all the lies you told and come up with more lies to cover up the first lie. Too complicated, my memory is not that good. But sometimes I have a lie all together, and ready to tell, but when the time comes, the Holy Ghost will have me stumble or I will have forgotten the lie I was going to tell. Now I don't even try any more. I just tell the truth, good or bad, and deal with the consequences.

You are light. God is the light of the world and we are light in Him. You are therefore His instrument to bring light to the world. Someone is always watching, even if you believe that God is that only someone. How you maintain that light is by seeking what is acceptable to God. Seek His face by studying the word and communing with Him. As you do so what is acceptable to Him will be revealed. You will recognize and quicken to His voice. You will understand His plan and thoughts towards you. Remember understanding is not a prerequisite for obedience. You do not have to understand your purpose to start doing. God requires your obedience whether you understand or not. However the more you commune with Him, He will give you understanding.

Fight for your happiness

For we do not wrestle against flesh and blood, but against principalities, against powers, against rulers of darkness of this age, against spiritual hosts of wickedness in the heavenly places. - Ephesians 6: 12

Happiness is spiritual warfare. It is tiresome to try to fight a spiritual fight in the flesh. How do we try to fight it in the flesh? By condemning ourselves. I have this and that, I should be happy. I'm doing this and that, I should be happy. I am living according to the word and doing what God told me to do, I should be happy. The flesh looks for a feeling of happiness; the spirit man chooses to be happy regardless.

Why are we not happy? The enemy tells us we are not good enough, or we are not doing enough. Happiness is not equated to action on our part. You have to know that you are good enough or that you are doing enough and CHOOSE to be happy. If the enemy can keep you in the "yes, but" category, he steals your joy. I have this but I'm missing that. I can do this but I can't do that. I'm doing what God told me to do, but I still don't have a husband/wife. Anything that follows the "but" cancels out what preceded it, because it is what followed the "but" that is the focus of our attention and energies.

So what's the answer? How do you fight for your happiness? It's simple, Praise Him. Do what you know to do, and give Him an about to praise for what you don't have. If God promised it, He will bring it to pass. Don't focus on the why or the timing. It's hard to be unhappy while praising God. So shout yourself happy.

Praise confuses the enemy. Praise obligates God to bless you. Praise shows God you are expecting a harvest. Praise keeps you focused on God rather than yourself. Praise shows your faithfulness to the process. Praise displays your trust in God.

Chapter 7
Living in the Moment

Which of you by worrying can add one cubit to his stature? ....Therefore do not worry about tomorrow, for tomorrow will worry about its own things. Sufficient for the day is its own trouble.
Matthew 6:25, 34

I have been pondering over this chapter for weeks now. That's generally my M.O. I could not grasp what God was trying to teach me in this section, so in fear I ran. I stopped reading and studying the word. Don't get me wrong, in theory I know what living in the moment means. I've heard the cliché: Live each day as your last. But in my head, it couldn't possibly be that simple. Plus a cliché is just that, something that sounds good in theory or on paper, but when putting it to action it is harder than you think.

I finally stopped running, that is a week before my deadline to finish this book. So what does it mean to live in the moment? Living in the moment is a state of mindfulness, which is intentional focus on the present. But how do you focus on the present? In chapter 1 I discussed the importance of letting go of the past. I am currently in graduate school pursuing my master's degree in counseling. For one of my assignments in my Clinical Counseling skills class I had to find a person to counsel for 3 sessions. I had a hard time finding someone so my classmate and I decided we would counsel each other. In my session when she was counseling me, she gave me an interesting homework assignment. She asked me to journal how I knew I was over my past, what steps did I take. Until that very moment I never really recognized I was actually over my past.

Let go of the past

To live in the moment you must first let go of the past. To be over the past does not mean, you never discuss it or have no memory of it. It doesn't even mean that all your feelings are resolved. I know that I am over my past because I don't dwell on it anymore. Letting go of the past is essential to living in the moment, because in order to get to the present you must get away from the past. What steps did I take?

1. **Acknowledge your feelings**

    As I stated in chapter 1, when I was molested I told myself a lot of things in order to protect myself from reliving the hurt. The one thing I remember telling myself over and over was "it was no big deal, all they did was touch me." Truth is I was a child and it was wrong for anyone to touch me in a sexual manner. And because I said it was no big deal, my mind was confused. I was hurting but I was telling myself it was wrong to feel hurt. So I went into a shell. I no longer trusted anyone and would not allow anyone to get close to me. As long as we hide our feelings we are unable to deal with them in a rational manner. Feelings come and go; it is how we deal with them that create lasting effects. I thought sex was love and therefore saw my body as a tool to get what I thought I was missing. Once I acknowledged my feelings I was able to allow myself to heal.

2. **Release the blame**

As I got older I had a lot of anger in me. I developed a "me against the world" attitude. I trusted no one. For a long time I blamed myself for the molestations. The first two I was 8 and 11 years old. They were both by women. I questioned my sexuality. I asked was I gay, is that why they chose me? I was a lonely child and had little friends. The girls befriended me when no one else would. I blamed myself because if I hadn't been seeking love then I would not have allowed it to happen. After all why didn't I tell anyone? Then I said they were children. Children don't just do such bad things, they learn by example. Just when I was getting over the first two, the third molestation happened when I was around 13. This one took me for a loop. I didn't know who to blame and this is where the anger set in. I was angry at the man for hurting me. I was angry at my mom, for not protecting me and getting me help. One day God spoke to me and told me to let go of the blame. After the molestation was a series of bad relationships of physical, verbal and emotional abuse. All of which I blamed myself because, again I was looking for love.

I am a person who accepts responsibility for my actions. If I mess up, I just deal with the consequences. In my mind unhappiness and emotional scars were my consequences. But God said I was blaming the wrong people. The girls were not the blame, because they were repeating behavior that they saw. Yes the man who molested me the third time was certainly at fault because he was an adult and I was a minor. But he was a pawn in a bigger scheme. My mother was not the blame, because she only handled the situation the best way she could. I was not the blame because I too was a child. So who is to blame I cried? God helped me see the big picture. The enemy used those people to try to stop me from getting to my future that God has for me. But God allowed it because it is the pain and experience of the past that He will use to free others.

3. **Forgive others and yourself**

Forgiveness is a big pill to swallow. Most feel like if they forgive they are letting the people who hurt them off the hook. Well here is another cliché. Forgiveness is for you not the ones who hurt you. Unforgiveness rots us from the inside out. We literally die on the inside and reflect bitterness and hate on the outside. The bible says we have to work out our own salvation with trembling and fear. What if the people we are mad at has asked God for forgiveness and moved on living a happy fulfilled life. You being miserable does not mean that they are miserable to. What helped me was I love to prove people wrong. If the trick of the enemy was to stop me from getting to my future, then I am not going to let him win by being stuck in the past. Forgiveness for me, as I said in chapter 1, was letting go that the past could have been any different. No matter how much I replayed the events over and over in my mind, I could not change it. There are no do-overs. So I asked myself how long I was going to allow it to hinder me from my dreams. While there are no do-overs, the new beginning comes when we see and use the pain as motivation.

4. **Realize others need your help**

When you can look back and see gratefulness for making it through as well as a purpose and blessing to help others. You are finally free from the past. I am literally an open book. I don't mind sharing my past experiences with others. In fact it brings me joy to see that people are listening and able to gain strength and encouragement from my testimony. In order to get here, we have to let go of the "why me" syndrome. God won't put more on us than we can bear. If He chose you, it is because He knew you could handle it.

I am able to be around the poor, homeless, destitute, rape victims, etc. and not be judgmental. I empathize with them and am able to remain humble, because it could have been me. Not only did God allow me to go through the painful things of my past but he allowed me to do so with my right mind. Victims of molestation can end up on the streets as prostitutes. Children from poverty and homes filled with abuse, drugs and alcohol can end up as drug addicts, alcoholics, teen mothers, or repeating the cycle living on welfare. But God chose me to be an example of how His grace and guidance could defy the odds and beat the statistics. I didn't have a child out of wedlock. I am not nor ever been on welfare in my adult life. I went to college and earned my degrees. I am still dreaming and have plenty more to accomplish.

Again to let go of the past does not mean to forget. But it means acknowledging the pain by being honest with yourself and dealing with your feelings. It means forgiving those who have harmed you as well as asking for forgiveness for those you have inflicted harm upon in an attempt to protect yourself. And it also means moving forward no longer allowing the past to hold you captive. Once the past no longer has a hold on you,

you are able to see past your hurt and begin to envision helping others.

Relinquish control of the future

In order to live in the present, we must not only let go of the past but also relinquish control of the future.

The Lord is not slack concerning His promise, as some count slackness, but is longsuffering toward us, not willing that any should perish but that all should come to repentance. - 2 Peter 3:9

I know that the above scripture is speaking of the return of the Lord. But it also speaks of the importance of holding on to the promises of God. None of us know the day or hour of His return therefore we live each day following the instructions of His word, repenting for our mistakes and waiting patiently for His return. During the wait it is important not to focus on the day of His return because it is out of our control.

To release control of the future we have to realize that we are unable to control it. There is no sense worrying about something that you can't control. Don't get me wrong planning for the future is totally different from worrying about the future. Planning is action oriented. You have to work to plan. Worrying is a thought process. We can't make anything happen by just thinking about it. The only thing that moves while we think is time. Before you know it valuable time has been wasted and nothing has been accomplished.

Releasing control is difficult to do, especially when the world is screaming "Take control." However as Christians we are followers of Christ, which means we trust Him to lead us in the right direction. In fact that is the difference between us and the rest of the world. The world is controlled by fleshly desires seeking what is gratifying to the flesh or what feels good. Christians, on the other hand, choose to follow God and walk in obedience seeking that which is pleasing to God.

As there were steps to let go of the past, there are also steps to release control of the future.

1. **Remember the word that was spoken over you**. If God has promised you something He will bring it to pass. We have to hold tight to those promises. The key is to seek God. Once He has promised you something, ask what steps you need to take to get there. I have said many times before: God is a God of order. He reveals things one step at a time. Once the first is completed the next will be revealed. We cannot get anxious for step two before we complete step one. Find joy in the expectancy of God's promise.

2. **Trust God's plan**. We have to realize that God knows best. Sometimes his plan may seem like the scenic route but it is the

best route. Have you ever searched for directions on map quest? Once you put in your starting location and the address of where you want to go, the site will sometimes ask whether you want the fastest route or the shortest distance. The fastest route usually includes the expressway, thus less traffic lights equals faster time. However the shortest distance, may be the street way, thus more traffic lights, and may take a few extra minutes to get there. The expressway may be the fastest route, but it can also be the most boring; the only scenery is other cars. It is impossible to enjoy the ride. I am an expressway girl. I can get anywhere on the expressway. But it speaks to my impatience. On the expressway I often experience road rage and anger at the other drivers for moving too slow. However when I choose to take the street route, I generally plan ahead by making sure I give myself some extra time to get to my destination because traffic moves at a slower pace. I also usually arrive at my destination a lot calmer and have even enjoyed the new businesses or even old business that I never paid any attention to that are in the neighborhoods. Think of the expressway as our own chosen route and the shortest distance as God's route. We may get there faster on the expressway but what have we seen and learned along the way? God's way may take longer but it teaches us patience and is the best preparation for what must happen once we reach our destination.

3. **Realize God is in control.** Worrying about the future is not our job. It's out of our control. We can't change it and there is nothing we can do or not do to manipulate its outcome. Our lives are completely ordained by God. There is nothing you can do that catches Him by surprise. It's not like God is in heaven, saying "Oh my, didn't know he/she was going to make that decision, got to change my plans." He knows every decision we made and are going to make. So why waste precious time worrying about something we can't change or control. Let God be God and focus on our job of following His instructions. Doing things our way just makes the road more difficult and may even extend the time of travel but it does not alter the route. Our decisions, good or bad, are just as God planned to get us to the Promised Land. This step is also important to help us eliminate self-condemnation. Sometimes we ponder on our mistakes too long thus extending our wilderness time, when we could just ask for forgiveness, forgive ourselves and move on.

4. **Stay in the word.** Read, pray, meditate and then pray some more. Sometimes we get so consumed with the cares of this world we forget to pray and seek God daily. Failure to commune with Him daily can lead to frustration, lack of hope, and bad choices. The bible says the steps of a righteous man

are ordered by the Lord. God cannot order our steps if we do not talk with Him. Relationship with God is the key to obtaining any promise or desire from God. The word reveals to us the mindset and thought process of the Lord. The word softens our heart and enables us to be receptive of His command. The word gives us the strength and ability to share His love with others. The word opens our spiritual eyes to the many promises and power of God. God reveals His character and conditional love for us in His word. Without the word the stresses of the world will consume us and leave us confused and full of worry. In the word there is peace and joy despite the destruction that is all around us. The more we commune with Him the more we recognize His voice and are able to quicken to His instruction. The Holy Spirit guides us according to the word, if we do not put the word in us, He cannot remind us of it in our time of need.

5. **Let go of fear**. *But He said to them, "why are you fearful, O you of little faith?" -Matthew 8:26*. What are you so afraid of? Fear and faith cannot coexist. Either you trust God or not. Either you believe the word or not. God has already given you the task. You know what to do. Yet you are still afraid. Tomorrow is not your concern. Please God by finishing today. One day at a time. Your dream is at hand, your purpose is calling you now. Your future is now. Yesterday is already gone and wasted. Why

continue to waste today worried about tomorrow. Tomorrow is not promised. At His word, tomorrow can cease to exist. We know that only God can make our dreams come true so why is it so hard to trust Him to do so. We are to fear God, not His purpose and plan for our life. As I stated earlier fear paralyzes us. By giving in to fear we are choosing to fail. We are incapable of success if we never try. The world says "it is better to try and fail than to not try at all." This may be a true statement, but as Christians we have the power and leadership of Jesus Christ, therefore in Him there is no failure.

Be mindful of the present

What is man that You are mindful of him, and the son of man that You visit him? - Psalm 8:4

To live in the moment is to be mindful of the present. In other versions "mindful" in Psalm 8 verse 4 is replaced with "think" and "visit" with "care. So if God is always thinking of us and caring for us, when we live in the past or future we are not on one accord with Him. God is not in our past and He is not waiting for us in the future. He is with us now. His thoughts are always on us and He is always concerned and caring for us.

To live in the moment is to be present with God in His thoughts concerning us today. Live each day seeking His guidance and what is pleasing to Him. I now understand the importance of beginning each day with prayer. But our prayers should not just be random or repetitive, as in "thank you Lord for waking me this morning..." Our prayers should be purposeful and seeking to get a step closer to our desires. We should ask Him to show us what he would have us to do each day and help us to keep our thoughts on Him.

He answered and said to them, "because it has been given you to know the mysteries of the kingdom of heaven, but to them it has not been given.
- Matthew 15:11

To live in the moment is to no longer doubt that you are in His will. No longer doubt that He is ordering your steps. It is the trick of the enemy to tell you that your dreams are not in His plans for you. It is the trick of the enemy to tell you that you are incapable of making your dreams come true. Accepting Christ as your Lord and Savior unlocked the mysteries of the kingdom. He reveals those mysteries through daily communication. You are in His will. Your thoughts are not His thoughts, but you have entered into a partnership with God through His word. You must trust Him and allow Him to lead you to those dreams. He knows the correct path. He knows the way to go. It may seem long and time consuming, but He knows what is best. There is no alternate route. Stop trying to run ahead. The journey seems long because you are dragging your feet. You are procrastinating on each step. Procrastination does not alter or eliminate the steps. They still must be completed in the order in which they were given. God is in control. Trust Him. Believe Him. Have faith in Him. No longer question every step. Just do it.

To live in the moment is to let go of your human thinking. Open your spiritual eyes and thoughts to be receptive of what God is doing and teaching. The steps that God has us taking may seem tedious and unproductive in providing immediate gratification. Sometimes in day to day tasks we can't see what God is doing. The world may pose a route that seemingly provides the instant happiness or success we desire. But God has to teach us that success is in Him, in the completion of each task rather than in the results or rewards. If we follow God and don't lose heart, we will certainly have plenty of rewards along the way.

To live in the moment is to wait for God's reward in expectancy. Decide whether you want recognition or reward. Do you want recognition from man or reward from God? God already recognizes you as His child, His birthright, therefore there is no greater recognition to be received or that can be given. We continue to seek recognition from man because we still have yet to recognize who we are in God. God's reward is beyond what man has, can give, or can see. God sees your pearls; he sees your beauty and will reward you accordingly.

Continuing to seek recognition from man is casting your pearls before swine. Your value is in your identity. Who do you say that you are? The child of a King behaves as such whether wearing a crown or not. Know that at the appointed time, the kingdom will be given to you. However the King must prepare you for ownership.

He said to them "But who do you say that I am?" - Matthew 16:15

In order to live in the moment you must believe in the "Great I Am" in you. Trust that the greater you want to become is available to you now through the one who lives in you. Just because you don't have what you want right now does not mean you are not capable of achieving it or worthy of receiving it.

Who you believe God to be is tied to your trust in Him. You lack trust because your thought process is one sided. You only think in terms of what you don't have. Be mindful of what you do have and have already accomplished. If you must, literally take inventory of your accomplishments. Type them up in a word document in large print. Print it out, make copies and post them in as many places as need be to remind you of what God has done. Post it at home on the bathroom mirror, on the fridge; in the car on the dash board; at work on your desk. Do whatever it takes to remind yourself that if God can do those things He can do even greater if you allow him.

Sometimes we take on more than we should because we will not allow God to be God in our lives or over our situations and circumstances. God is a gentleman, if you want Him to open your door you must step aside, wait, and allow Him to do so. You are not alone. It is not you against the world. God can make the world your footstool all He requires is trust and faith in Him.

So Jesus stood still and called them and said "what do you want Me to do for you?" - Matthew 20:32

What do you want God to do for you? Let go of the materialistic desires and honestly answer this question. You are His child. His desire is to please you. Tell Him what you truly want. Make another list of your wants. Pray about it and watch Him fulfill. Devote Christians will say that serving God is not about receiving, I agree to a certain extent. If the only reward in serving God is going to heaven, then what happiness is there to look forward to while living on Earth? Fulfilling your purpose is a reward. Purpose is followed by gifting. Every good and perfect gift comes from God.

To live in the moment is to accept God's choice of you. He already loves you. He already chose you. There is nothing you can do or say to change His mind. Accept Him; accept His choice and you will be able to accept yourself. Don't question it, just accept it and say YES. Stop asking "why me." Why not you? He chose you at birth. He has been with you since birth. He has been waiting on you to acknowledge Him and allow Him to take the lead. Life will be much easier if you just accept the call and accept His instructions. Rebellion takes up a lot of time and energy. By the time we stop running, we are too tired to take another step. Allow God to rejuvenate you. Don't worry about the time you spent running or how long you were running, for there is a lesson in every journey. Thank God for opening your eyes, now the only thing left to do is follow Him.

Chapter 8
Enjoy Who You Are & Where You Are With God

Now may the God of hope fill you with all joy and peace in believing, that you may abound in hope by the power of the Holy Spirit.
Romans 15:13

Your joy is contingent upon the source of your hope and belief. Likewise your identity is contingent upon that same hope and belief. God is the center of our joy and in whom we place our hopes. There is peace in knowing that God, whom never fails and makes all things possible, is leading us to our destiny.

And Jesus answered and said to them "Take heed that no one deceives you." - Matthew 24:4

No longer allow the enemy to make you question who you are. You know your purpose. You have your instructions. Walk in them and rest in assurance that you are in God's will. Stop worrying about the how, when and why. Stop being concerned about the final destination. The journey is just as important.

Peace brings joy. Be excited to complete each task and look forward to the next.

Who are you?

We are all God's children. The sole purpose of all Christians is to build and edify the kingdom. The uniqueness of your creation is in the "how" will you edify and build the kingdom. By now you should know the broad definition of the how. However the details will be revealed in the journey. Write down your purpose and read it every day. Each day ask God to show you how to fulfill it. This is an important step to acknowledging who you are. If you don't repeat it every day, the enemy will throw obstacles and people in your way to confuse you. Where there is confusion there is no action. If you are unsure about who you are you will be stagnant and unable to be used by God. Repeating it every day helps it get into your heart and spirit and no one will be able to convince you otherwise.

To fulfill your purpose you must allow God to lead you into the unknown, never seen before territory. Though you may not have had an example, you are the example for others. The more you trust God, the higher He will take you. A husband/wife, career, or whatever you are believing God for are just the beginning. Unless you plan on dying after receiving those things, God has a lot more in store for you.

Success is all over you! Each day that you choose to follow God, you are successful. Each day that you choose to allow God to uncover His abilities in you, you are successful. Success is not in material possession but in doing what God created you to do. Success is God's vision coming to pass, not your own vision of what your life should be or should have been. You are beautiful, strong, intelligent and talented. You have yet to see the capabilities God has placed in you. Rather than fear what is to come, fear what will not become if you remain in fear. Thy will be done on Earth as it is in Heaven.

Indiana Tuggle

"Our Greatest Fear"

Our greatest fear is not that we are inadequate,
our deepest fear is that we are powerful beyond measure.

It is our light, not our darkness, that most frightens us.
We ask ourselves, who am I to be brilliant,
gorgeous, handsome, talented and fabulous?

Actually, who are you not to be?
You are a child of God.

Your playing small does not serve the world.
There is nothing enlightened about shrinking
so that other people won't feel insecure around you.

We were born to make manifest the glory of God that is
within us.
It is not just in some of us; it is in everyone.

And, as we let our own light shine, we unconsciously
give
other people permission to do the same.
As we are liberated from our fear,
our presence automatically liberates others.

Author: Marianne Williamson, from her book "A Return to Love"

Don't allow fear to keep you from being the best you can be.

If you want something you've never had, you must be willing to do something you've never done. – Thomas Jefferson

I believe that people who look back on life with regret do so because of fear. Fear allowed them to miss opportunities or cowered them to accept less than they deserved. In tackling fear we have to beware of "wolves in sheep's clothing." The things we want from God require our patience. It is important during the journey to keep a close relationship with Him. The enemy will send imposters. I know this oh too well.

In my loneliness I was longing for someone to spend time with, to go out on a date, etc. I met a guy. Well actually he was a friend of a friend. Honestly when I saw him for the first time, when I looked at him I saw the devil. Not that I know what the devil looks like but there was an evil presence about him. I ignored it; I was vulnerable and got involved with him anyway. I ignored all the signs that he was not completely what I wanted or deserved and got involved with him anyway. It was great at first, he was giving me all that I thought I was missing. He wanted to spend time with me every day.

From the day of our first conversation we were inseparable. We saw each other daily, I left work and went straight to his house. When I was at work he texted me all day and we talked on my breaks. We even went out two to three times a week. But then things went too far. One night while watching a movie at my place we had sex. I felt horrible, I had broken 5 years of celibacy. But I thought I was in love.

What did I ignore? I ignored that he was living at home with his mother. He just moved back to town and needed time to adjust I said. I ignored that he had not had a traditional job in over 5 years and was therefore behind on his child support. He is a contractor and building a business takes time I said. I also ignored the fact that he was content with his situation. He didn't see anything wrong with his life and in fact thought he was a good catch and would make a great husband. I even ignored that he moved back in town because of a failed marriage, that he says was all her fault because she didn't "believe" in him and only thought about money.

Honestly it was not my place to say that there was a problem with him. But the true problem was, he was not the one for me, he was not what I needed and deserved. Because of my impatience I jumped into a relationship with the wrong person. Because we had sex, I felt it was too late and that I couldn't let go. We even planned to get married. But thankfully because of close friends, a great pastor/father figure and my own personal relationship with God I called the relationship off before it was truly too late.

After that I was truly thankful that God cared enough about me to not allow me to make the biggest mistake of my life. My fear of being alone almost caused me a life of misery. It took me a couple of months to forgive myself, but I finally did and realized that God knows what's best for us. His best is far beyond what we could even dream of. Sometimes I may be lonely, as I am only human, but I am never alone. I have God and great friends in my life. I am discovering me and enjoying the process. When Mr. Right finally comes along, there will be a better me for him to love and cherish.

Whose are you?

Nevertheless He saved them for His name's sake, that He might make His mighty power known. - Psalm 106:8

Once we accept that Jesus died on the cross for our sins, His shed blood makes us His name sake. So why then do we allow the enemy to confusion us thus robbing us of our inheritance? If we do not accept that we belong to Him we cannot walk in the power of Him who lives in us. God has given us all authority. However authority without acknowledgement or ownership is useless.

God is our Father, we must believe that and walk in the power and authority that comes along with it. God does not forget and we also should not forget or ever doubt. This is important because one of the greatest power of authority we receive as children of God is the power of the tongue. The bible states life and death are in the power of the tongue. In fact there are many scriptures regarding how what we say has the power to change the atmosphere. Whether it be good or bad, what we say shall be done. Therefore we should use this power carefully and with boldness.

Boldness comes from knowing with certainty whose you are. Remember the story of the withered fig tree. Jesus was hungry, he saw the fig tree from afar but when he approached it there was no fruit, only leaves. He spoke "let no fruit grow on you ever again" and immediately the fig tree withered away. Later He explained to the disciples that if you have faith and do not doubt you can do the same. Therefore anything that is not bearing fruit in our lives we have the power to curse it and make it wither away like the fig tree. We must believe that whatever we ask for in prayer He will do it.

Now this is the confidence that we have in Him, that if we ask anything according to His will, He hears us. And if we know that He hears us, whatever we ask, we know that we have the petitions that we have asked of Him. - 1 John 5: 14 – 15

The enemy easily destroys this confidence when we fall into temptation. We heavily condemn ourselves by thinking that God is punishing us or that our mess up was so horrible that God is angry with us. God does not disown us because of our sin. In fact it is the reverse. We disown God when we sin. The longer we wallow in pity, not asking for forgiveness or not believing we have been forgiven we have given up our authority. Are there consequences to our mistakes? Absolutely! But it is by grace that we are saved and by His mercy that He forgives us and casts our mistakes as far as the east is from the west. Repent and keep moving forward. Don't allow the enemy to trip you up and slow down God's plan for your life by holding tight to your mistakes. I once heard Steve Harvey say it's only a mistake if you don't learn from it, if you learn from it, its education and education is priceless.

Remember who you are in everything that you do or say. Don't allow anyone to challenge your identity. When things aren't happening the way you want them to or as fast as you want them to, remember God is not slack concerning you and His word will not return to Him void. If we daily commune with Him and pray about everything, God will make known to us the traps of the enemy. This does not mean, as Christians we will never struggle, but it does mean that God will always be with us and working everything out for our good.

Indiana Tuggle

Enjoy where you are

I know this is a cliché but it is true: Life is a Journey! Sometimes the best moments in life happen not when we are experiencing them but rather when we reflect back on them. Don't be so anxious for life to speed up so that you can receive a certain thing or obtain a certain status. In doing so we miss the journey and the lessons they teach.

His Lord said to Him, 'Well done, good and faithful servant, you have been faithful over a few things, I will make you ruler over many things. Enter into the joy of your Lord." - Matthew 25:23

Your faithfulness is required to receive joy. Joy is not a result of success; it is a result of God's faithfulness and promise to you. If you do what God called you to do, He promises joy. If you complete the tasks He assigned you to do, He promises joy. Greater is coming with every step you take. Have faith in God and He will give you joy. Joy begins with knowing that following God is the right path. It is when we rely on our own understanding or our own strength that frustration comes. Regardless of how difficult it may seem, continue to follow God. There are no wrong turns or regrets with God. Disobedience produces regret. Continue to trust Him and believe the word spoken over you.

Your past or your future is not the source of your joy, nor are they predictors of your destiny. Society likes to predict the future of the next generation based on environment, education, income level or status of parents, and the mistakes one makes. But the moment we accepted Jesus, as our Lord and Savior, we became unpredictable. At that moment we got back on the road God meant for us at creation.

Your joy is in your present with God. Joy does not come when you reach a certain level or pass a certain test. Joy is available now. However patience is a prerequisite. We must not get weary in well doing and wait patiently on the Lord. I said earlier that the wait is for us, not God. We are not waiting on God, we are waiting on the appointed time. Remember God does not move out of season.

God is time, therefore it will not run out before His promises are fulfilled. In fact give Him your time (praying, studying the word, etc.) and He will pause time for you. What's the point of having success if we do not have health and strength to enjoy it? If we wait on the Lord, and act according to His will, He will ensure we are able to enjoy what He has in store for us. God is the best age defying solution ever. No cream can do what abiding in Jesus Christ can. Greater will wait for you. Love will wait for you.

God knows your value. Sometimes the world does not know how valuable a person is until they are gone, like an artist whose paintings become more valuable after their death. But did they allow lack of popularity to cause them to stop painting? You must know who you are in order to do the work. Passion produces joy, and passion is birthed from purpose.

Nothing pleases God more than obedience to His will. The bible says all God's promises are yes and Amen. (2 Corinthians 1:20) We don't have to fully understand to be obedient. We cannot serve God through logic. We worship Him in spirit and truth. We serve Him with our whole heart. Allow your heart that has been hardened by the pains of the world, to be softened through the love of Christ.

Choose to abide in happiness. Regardless of what happens or does not happen, choose to rejoice in the fact that God has you here for a reason. God promises to give us the desires of our heart if we trust in Him. Stop focusing on what you don't have, and focus on the task in front of you now. What does God want you to do now? I'm sure it does not involve complaining and whining about Mr. or Mrs. Right. Right now you have work to do. You will soon realize that once you get busy working and take your mind off Mr. or Mrs. Right, they are right around the corner. We cannot expect the things that are coming to us on the journey to come when we are standing still or sitting on our butts watching TV.

God has equipped us with everything we need to obtain the promises He made. It is not His fault if we settle for less than what we deserve. How bad do you want it, him or her? Remember nothing is worth having unless you put in the work. If God handed it to you right now, would you be able to handle it? Most of us would say yes, but only God really knows. Relax. Be patient and allow God to show you the way. His way is always best and His way is the fullness of joy.

When you are becoming impatient with waiting or the enemy tries to steal your joy remember these verses:

Habakkuk 2:3
For the vision is yet for an appointed time; but at the end it will speak, and it will not lie. Though it tarries, wait for it; because it will surely come, it will not tarry.

Hebrews 10:23
Let us hold fast the confession of our hope without wavering, for He who promised is faithful.

Hebrews 3:14
For we have become partakers of Christ if we hold the beginning of our confidence steadfast to the end,

Isaiah 40:31
But those who wait on the Lord shall renew their strength; hey shall mount up with wings like eagles, they shall run and not be weary, they shall walk and not faint.

John 15: 11
These things I have spoken to you, that My joy may remain in you, and that your joy may be full

Psalm 118: 24

This is the day the Lord has made; we will rejoice and be glad in it

Psalm 130:5
I wait for the Lord, my soul waits, and in His word I do hope.

Psalm 145:15-16
The eyes of all look expectantly to You, and You give them their food in due season. You open Your hand and satisfy the desire of every living thing

Psalm 27: 14
Wait on the Lord; be of good courage, and He shall strengthen your heart; wait, I say, on the Lord!

Psalm 33:20
Our soul waits for the Lord; He is our help and our shield.

Psalm 45:7
You love righteousness and hate wickedness; therefore God, Your God, has anointed You with the oil of gladness more than Your companions

Psalm 5: 11 – 12
But let all those rejoice who put their trust in You; Let them ever shout for joy, because You defend them; Let those also who love Your name be joyful in You. For You, O Lord, will bless the righteous; with favor You will surround him as with a shield.

Psalm 51: 12-13
Restore to me the joy of Your salvation, and uphold me by Your generous Spirit. Then I will teach transgressors Your ways, and sinners shall be converted to You.

Psalm 62:5
My soul, wait silently for God alone, for my expectation is from Him.

Romans 14: 17-18
For the kingdom of God is not eating and drinking, but righteousness and peace and joy in the Holy Spirit. For he who serves Christ in these things is acceptable to God and approved by men.

www.ingramcontent.com/pod-product-compliance
Lightning Source LLC
Chambersburg PA
CBHW021128300426
44113CB00006B/333